South African Tribes and their History

Race and Ethnic Influences

Author

Joshua Berry

Copyright Notice

Copyright © 2017 Global Print Digital
All Rights Reserved

First Printing: 2017.

ISBN: 978-1-912483-14-3

Publisher: Global Print Digital.
Arlington Row, Bibury, Cirencester GL7 5ND
Gloucester
United Kingdom.
Website: www.homeworkoffer.com

Table of Content

Introduction

South Africa is one of the most geographically varied countries of the African continent, comprising territory that ranges from the rolling, fertile plains of the highveld and the wide open savanna of the Eastern Transvaal to the Kalahari Desert and the peaks of the Drakensberg Mountains. While all of its diverse regions offer ample opportunities for adventure travel, the focus in South Africa as in much of sub-Saharan Africa is the safari.

In addition to possessing two of the world's most renowned wildlife reserves, the Kruger and the Kalahari Gemsbok National Parks, the country contains over a dozen smaller regional parks and reserves. In addition, with its excellent road and rail systems, its abundance of top-rated accommodations, and its bountiful farmlands and vineyards, South Africa allows visitors ample opportunity for more luxurious comfort along with adventuresome excitement.

South Africa is located, as one might expect, on the southern tip of Africa. It is bordered by the Atlantic Ocean on the west, the Indian Ocean on the south and east. Along its northern border, from west to east, lie Namibia, Botswana, and Zimbabwe, and to the northeast are Mozambique and Swaziland. Wholly-enclosed by South Africa, and situated in its eastern central plain, is the independent kingdom of Lesotho.

Almost all of South Africa's 472,000 square miles (1.2 million sq. km.) lie below the Tropic of Capricorn, and the country is geographically composed of three primary regions: an expansive central plateau, a nearly continuous escarpment of mountain ranges that ring the plateau on the west, south, and east, and a narrow strip of low-lying land along the coast. Most of the central plateau (and most of the country) consists of high (4,000-6,000 ft/1,220-1,830 m), rolling grassland known as highveld. The highest points of the mountainous escarpment are found in the stunning Drakensberg (dragon's back) Mountains, where the tips of dragon's back can exceed heights of 10,000 ft (3,050 m).

In the northwest, South Africa's Kalahari Gemsbok National Park, one of the continent's largest game reserves, extends into the red sands and scrub grasslands of the great Kalahari Desert. In the northeast, the highveld plateau descends to the Bushveld and Limpopo River basins. The Bushveld comprises South Africa's extensive savanna, in which is found the country's marvelously rich and diverse game reserve, the world-renowned Kruger National Park.

Although South Africa's climate varies considerably across its various regions and environments, temperatures remain comfortable throughout the year. The best time to visit for safari is between May to August, when there is less rain and much less dense vegetation, making animal sightings far more frequent.

South Africa's population of forty million is three-quarters black (African) and about 15% white (European), with the remaining 10% comprised of people of mixed white, Malayan, and black descent and people of Asian (mostly Indian) descent. The African majority is composed of many different ethnic groups, the largest of which are Zulu, Xhosa, Tswana, and Bapedi. Until very recently, the country's racial divisions were harshly enforced as part of the government's official policy of Apartheid, or apartness. Although the government began to dismantle apartheid in 1989 after prolonged resistance, protest, and international economic sanctions, racial inequality remains

South African Race and ethnicity, an issue

Race and ethnicity have been and still is at the heart of South African history, politics, society and economy since the European colonization. South Africa remains a complex mix of different races, cultural identities, languages and ethnic bonds. During the colonial times, the Dutch East Indian introduced racial segregation. In 1795 the British took over the Cape of Good Hope, and they continue with racial segregation. The concept of race became a particularly explosive idea during colonization, as well as during the Apartheid period which begun in 1948. Race is defined as a social concept referring to a group of people who share distinct and similar physical characteristics.

During the apartheid period, the government introduced numerous legislations based on racial classification. For example, the legislative basis for racial classification during apartheid was the Population Registration Act No. 30 of 1950. This Act divided the South African population into three main racial groups: Whites, Natives (Blacks), Indians and Coloured people (people of mixed race). Race was used for political, social and economic purposes. Politically, White people had the rights to vote, access to state security and protection as well as representation in the National Assembly as compared to people. Economically, Whites had the privilege of having access to much more skilled and office jobs, and they had access to own the productive land and other means of productions.

The other apartheid legislations were the Group Areas Act of 1950 and Prohibition of Mixed Marriages Act of 1949. The Group Areas Act put an end to diverse areas and determined where one lived according to race. Each race was allocated its own area, which was used in later years as a basis for forced removals. The Prohibition of Mixed Marriages Act of 1949 did not allow marriage between persons of different races, and the Immorality Act of 1950 made sexual relations with a person of a different race a criminal offence.

Similarly, the Reservation of Separate Amenities Act of 1953 legalised the racial segregation of public services, premises and other amenities. For example, municipal grounds were reserved for a particular race, creating, among other things, separate beaches, buses, hospitals, schools and universities. Blacks were provided with services greatly inferior to those of Whites, and, to a lesser degree, to those of Indian and Coloured people. The Bantu Education Act of 1953 legalised racial separation of education in South Africa. A separate system of education was crafted for Black South African students and it was designed to prepare Black people for lives as a labouring class. In 1959 separate universities were created for Black, Coloured and Indian people. Existing universities were not permitted to enrol new Black students.

Ethnicity

Before colonisation and apartheid in South Africa, the concept of ethnicity was rooted in the ideas of bonds in kinship, biology and ancestry. Ethnicity has been associated with the belief that ethnic groups are extended kinship networks that serve as basic dividing lines within societies, embracing groups differentiated by colour, language, religion and race. In South Africa, ethnicity involved more visible local communities, built on face to face signal of dialect, kinship, status, religion, cultural practices, and on the force of understanding and fear produced by rural isolation.

Ethnicityrefers to shared cultural practices, perspectives, and distinctions that set apart one group of people from another. The most common characteristics distinguishing various ethnic groups are ancestry, territorial possession, language, forms of dress, a sense of history and religion. These characteristics were the units of social, economic and political organisations and inter-communal relations. Ethnic differences are not inherited; they are *learned*. South Africa consists of different ethnic groups located in different rural homelands. They were peasants or self-providing groups and their economy was agriculture. Land was important to the reproduction of social and economic life.

During the colonial and apartheid periods, the Black population of South Africa was divided into major ethnic groups; namely Nguni people which consisted of: Zulu, Xhosa, Ndebele and Swazi, Sotho people which consisted of Northern Sotho (Bapedi), Southern Sotho (Basotho) and Tswana, Shangaan-Tsonga and Venda, as well as Coloured and Afrikaans. There were separate Bantustans for the Zulus, Xhosas, Sothos, Tswanas, Vendas, Pedis and Shangaans. In urban areas, Africans were housed in the urban townships on ethnic lines and received their schooling in ethnic schools. Indians, Coloureds and Africans were also allotted separate schools.

The largest ethnic group in South Africa is the Zulu and the majority of them live in KwaZulu Natal Province and Gauteng Province. The second largest is the Xhosa group; they are located in the Eastern

Cape Province and Western Cape Province. South African ethnic groups are also found across South Africa's boundaries in neighbouring countries. For example, Nguni-speaking Swazi people make up almost the entire population of Swaziland. At least 1.3 million Sesotho speakers live in Lesotho, and more than 1 million people in Botswana speak Tswana. Tsonga and related languages speakers live in Mozambique, and Venda is also spoken by several thousand people in Southern Zimbabwe.

One of the main characteristics of ethnicity is language. In South Africa, there are more than ten languages and others are grouped as Nguni and Sotho languages. IsiZulu, isiXhosa, siSwati and isiNdebele are Nguni languages. Sepedi (Northern Sotho), Sesotho (Southern Sotho) and Setswana (Tswana) are Sotho-Tswana languages. Venda and Tsonga are the other two official languages in South Africa. English and Afrikaans are also official languages spoken in South Africa.

The majority of the White population, about 60 percent is Afrikaans, with many of the remaining 40 percent being of British or European descent. The Coloured population has a mixed lineage, which often comprises the indigenous Khoisan people and White settlers. Most of the Coloured population live in the Northern and Western Cape Provinces, whilst the majority of the Indian population live in KwaZulu-

Natal. The Afrikaner population is especially concentrated in the Gauteng and Free State Provinces.

The apartheid government ended in 1994 and was replaced by the Constitutional democracy. South Africa is a multi-racial democratic country which embraces its diversity. Symbolically, the image of the 'Rainbow Nation', made popular by Archbishop Desmond Tutu in 1994, is the most important symbols used to promote the ideology of a free, multiracial democratic society. Other symbols include the constitutional recognition of eleven official languages.

The South African Constitution provides equal human, political and social rights to all individuals regardless of race, ethnicity or language. All adult South African citizens have the right to vote and hold office. Section 9.3 of the Bill of Rights in the Constitution of the Republic of South Africa states that the "state may not unfairly discriminate directly or indirectly" on grounds including race, colour, ethnic or social origin, culture or language. a subsection of the same section further states that "discrimination on one or more of the grounds listed in subsection (3) is unfair unless it is established that the discrimination is fair" and sections of the Bill of Rights and the broader Constitution also states that 'the nation' is committed to ensuring redress for past racially discriminatory policies.

Act 1970, of the Black Homeland Citizenship

During Apartheid, starting from the late 1950s the South African Government attempted to divide South Africa into a number of separate states, called homelands, for Blacks. Under the homeland system, each state was supposed to develop into a separate nation-state for a different ethnic group. According to the Promotion of Bantu Self-Government Act No. 46 of 1959, Black people were classified into ethnic groups for whom a so-called homeland would be established. Approximately thirteen per cent of the land which represented fifty per cent of South Africa's arable land was reserved and divided into ten Black "homelands" amongst eight ethnic units (Davenport, 1977: p. 268).

The Black Homeland Citizenship Act 26 of 1970 (assent gained 26 March), subsequently renamed the Black States Citizenship Act, 1970 and the National States Citizenship Act, 1970, was a denaturalization law which was instrumental to this effect and required that all South African Blacks become citizens of one of the self-governing territories. The law declaredBlack people as aliens in urban areas, and could only live there after receiving special permission. It changed the status of Black people living in South Africa so that they were no longer citizens of South Africa, but became citizens of one of the ten autonomous territories. According to the law, "No Black person will eventually qualify [for South African nationality and the right to work or live in South Africa] because they will all be aliens, and as such, will only be able to occupy the houses bequeathed to them by their fathers, in the urban areas, by special permission of the Minister." (Connie Mulder, South African Information and Interior Minister, 1970.)

Four of the states were given independence (Transkei, Ciskei, Bophuthatswana and Venda), although this was never recognised by any other country. Each homeland was supposed to develop into a separate-nation state within which the eight Black ethnic groups were to find and grow their separate national identity, culture and language. The aim was to strip Blacks of their South African citizenship and ensure a demographic majority of White people within South Africa by having all ten Bantustans achieve full independence. In addition, urban townships were established to provide a readily available supply of labour, but had to be far enough away enough from white residential areas

The Homelands were:

Transkei

Fighting related to Transkei Independence breaks out in Umtata, December, 1976. Source: Photograph by Chris Van der Merwe © BAHA

An early history of the Transkei area

Originally the Transkei included the territories of Idutywa Reserve, Fingoland (Mfenguland) and Galekaland (Gcalekaland). Following their annexation they were restructured into the divisions of Butterworth, Tsomo and Nqamakwe for Fingoland; Kentani and Willowvale for Galekaland; and Idutywa for the Idutywa Reserve.

The alienation of Xhosa ancestral lands began during the 1770s when the Dutch annexed the border areas between the Gamtoos and Bushman's Rivers and began a gradual process of agrarian settlement that misrepresented indigenous concepts of land ownership. These incursions began to take on a more military aspect after the British annexation of the Cape Colony in 1806.

After the annexation the eastern frontier of the Cape became the arena for a series of increasingly bitter land wars. In 1811 and 1812 the British expelled the Xhosa people from the Zuurveld and annexed it to the Cape as the District of Albany. Following further clashes in 1818 and 1819 a highly contentious meeting was held on 14 October 1819 between the Cape Governor, Lord Charles Somerset, and Ngqika, paramount Chief of the amaRharhab. They concluded a verbal treaty which left the Xhosa no alternative but to yield the fertile region between the Great Fish and the Keiskamma Rivers. Initially this was known as the Neutral Territory, but in time it began to be referred to as the Ceded Territory and was settled by European farmers and their Khoikhoi allies.

In 1829 the area was annexed to the Cape and in 1833 amendments were made to its border, sparking off the frontier war of 1834 and 1835. On 21 December 1834 the Xhosa attacked the eastern regions of the Cape, and swept, virtually unchecked across the districts of Victoria and Albany, reaching the Sunday's River, near Uitenhage and Port Elizabeth. The Xhosa were, however, not interested in the re-occupation of their former territories so much as in the return of captured cattle to their lands over the Keiskamma River. Consequently, in January 1835, they began to fall back with he British on their heels.

On 31 March 1835 the British invaded Xhosa territory east of the Keiskamma River and on 10 May Governor D'Urban extended the colonial boundaries to the Great Kei River. On 16 June this area was proclaimed the Province of Queen Adelaide. The two parties concluded peace treaties on 17 September 1835 whereby the amaNgqika, amaNdlambe and amaGqunukhwebe were allotted specific territories within the province. They still gave over the greater part of their lands to the Cape Colony for European occupation. This included a strip of Gcaleka land east of the Great Kei River around Kei Drift and Butterworth.

The Colonial Office in London did not support these developments, and on 5 December 1836 the proclamation of the Province, as well as all treaties arising from it, were declared null and void, and the eastern frontier was returned to the Keiskamma River. Following the frontier war from 1846 to 1848, better known as the War of the Axe, the Ceded Territory was proclaimed the Division of Victoria on 23 December 1847, and on the same day the proclamation of British Kaffraria pushed the Cape-Xhosa boundary line to the Great Kei River, thereby returning it to its position in 1836.

This was extended in 1848 by the annexation of additional territory between the White Kei and Black Kei Rivers, later to become the

Division of Queenstown. In December 1850 the amaNgqika rose in revolt. They were defeated in 1853 and a complex re-allocation of lands with "friendly" groups being allocated land in British Kaffraria while rebel clans were banished east of the Kei River, was initiated.

European settlement of this region was stepped up in 1857 with the arrival of German and British groups. In 1857 the so-called "cattle killing" led to the starvation, and ultimate death of some 70 000 Xhosa people. In a brief period of 6 months their numbers were reduced from 105 000 to 37 200 persons. This effectively brought their armed resistance to European colonialism in the eastern Cape to an end. Barring a brief revolt in 1877 and 1878, when the amaGcaleka turned upon their amaMfengu neighbours, the British annexation of lands east of the Kei River was able to proceed unimpeded.

In 1866 British Kaffraria was annexed to the Cape Colony. In September 1879 this was followed by Idutywa Reserve and Mfenguland, and Gcalekaland in 1885. It is assumed that the restructuring of these territories into the divisions of Butterworth, Idutywa, Kentani, Nqamakwe, Tsomo and Willowvale dates from these times.

While the official annexation of territory was proceeding, the European population of lands north of the Great Kei River was growing rapidly. By the mid-1880's they numbered nearly 10 000 and in 1882 White farmers were beginning to settle illegally in Emigrant Thembuland, Thembuland Proper and parts of the Gatberg district of Griqualand East, later known as the Division of Maclear, which had become depopulated as the result of the frontier wars. European settlement was further assisted by the Thembu chief Ngangelizwe who opened up Maxongo's Hoek, in the Division of Slang River, to White farmers. In 1882 he also sold land in the district of Umtata for White use.

Other European settlers were purchasing land in the districts of the Indwe River, Kokstad and Matatiele, while tracts of land in Galekaland were surveyed for White ownership. The following census figures are available for the territory:

DIVISION	pop 1891	lit'cy	pop 1904	lit'cy
TRANSKEI, territory of	153 563	6 941	177 730	18 582
Division of Butterworth	15 312	1 344	19 202	2 810
Division of Idutywa	25 707	573	27 593	1 535
Division of Kentani	29 026	483	34 238	1 983
Division of Nqamakwe	30 442	2 550	34 234	5 906
Division of Tsomo	16 663	968	20 034	3 207

Division of Willowvale	36 413	1 023	42 429	3 071

The Transkei homeland

The Transkei region was the scene of various attempts to establish segregated districts before the period of apartheid. The Glen Gray Act of 1894 saw the establishment of district councils under the leadership of chiefs. The idea of using chiefs as proxy rulers eventually became a cornerstone of the Bantustan policy of the apartheid government, announced in 1959.

Under the Bantu Authorities Act of 1951, the Transkei became, in 1959, the first region to be established as a Territorial Authority; and in 1963 it became the first Bantustan to be granted 'self-government'. The area was divided into three physically seperate regions and took up approximately 43 798 square kilometres. Due to it's proximity to the Drakensberg Mountain Range it was extremely mountainius. Kaiser Matanzima, appointed Chief of the AmaHala clan in 1940, supported and promoted the apartheid concept of separate development and played a crucial role in the politics of the homeland.

Although chief of the AmaHala, his authority was subject to the overrule of the Paramount Chief of the Tembu, Sabata Dalindyebo, who opposed the Bantu Authorities system. Matanzima entered the

Transskei Territorial Authority (known as the Bunga) in 1955, and grew to become the favourite of apartheid's social engineers. To bypass the authority of Dalindyebo, they appointed him Regional Chief of Emigrant Tembuland in 1958, and in 1966 consolidated the position by making him Paramount Chief of the Emigrant Tembu, thus making him Dalindyebo's equal.

The constitution of the Transkei, drawn up in Pretoria under the watchful eye of Prime Minister Hendrik Verwoerd, determined that the Transkei cabinet was to be elected by ballot in the Legislative Assembly. It would control the following portfolios: Justice, Finance, Education, the Interior, Agriculture and Forestry, and Roads and Works.

The Assembly comprised the four Paramount Chiefs of the Transkei, 60 chiefs from regional authorities, and 45 members who would be elected in general elections. Although most of those elected were supporters of Paramount Chiefs Sabata Dalindyebo of Tembuland and Victor Poto of Western Pondoland, Kaiser Matanzima held sway over the legislature through the support of chiefs aligned to him. Matanzima was thus appointed Chief Minister of the Transkei, a 'self-governing territory within the Republic of South Africa'.

In elections, held before the status of self-government was conferred in 1963, Matanzima's Transkeian National Independence Party (TNIP) was defeated by the Democratic Party, which called for multiracialism, common South African citizenship and opposition to the Bantustan system. The DP won 33 of the 45 seats, but Matanzima received the support of 42 of the 58 government-appointed chiefs, and was appointed Chief Minister. Led by Knowledge Guzana, the DP lost its following over the next few years because of Matanzima's campaign to destroy the party in which members were often detained and banned.

When elections were held in1973, the TNIP won a majority of seats as well as votes, and Guzana was replaced in 1976 by Hector Ncokazi, who was influenced by the Black Consciousness Movement.

Matanzima's rule and the apartheid regime had been opposed by more radical forces long before this. In the early 1960s, the PAC's armed wing, Poqo, launched several attempts to assassinate Matanzima, all of which failed. But Poqo succeeded in killing one of Matanzima's advisors in October 1962. They also killed Tembu Chief GwebindalaMabuza in October and Chief MagezaDalasile in December.

Matanzima ran a brutal regime, and using the infamous Proclamation R400, neutralized all opposition through bannings and detentions. The proclamation had been put in place to deal with the intense rural resistance to apartheid in Pondoland in 1960.

Matanzima developed an effective working knowledge of the Bantu Authorities system, and agitated for independence. He mounted a vigorous campaign to promote his homeland, pressuring the government to have border districts incorporated into the Transkei, and in 1972 he pushed for the amalgamation of all Xhosa territory, including the Ciskei, under his leadership.

In 1976 Transkei became the first of the four homelands to be granted independence. Supported by the South African government, Matanzima managed to overshadow rivals such as Dalindyebo, despite the latter's greater support among the people in the area. Matanzima ruled the Transkei as Prime Minister, with his brother George occupying the position of Minister of Justice.

One of George Matanzima's first acts as Justice Minister was to detain John Kani and Winston Ntshona when they performed Athol Fugard's *SizweBansi is Dead* in Umtata. The actors were released following demonstrations in New York by well-known performers.

Despite his demands for more territory and his disputes with the South African government, Matanzima maintained power with the help of Pretoria and legislation modeled on the South African system.

Between April 1978 and April 1980, Matanzima engaged in a dispute over the status of Griqualand East, and broke off diplomatic ties with the apartheid government, and threatened an end to the 'non-aggression pact'. Weeks later, with its economy bankrupt, the homeland was forced to accept a bail-out of R73-million from the diplomatically alienated South African government.This grant was in addition to an annual grant of, R113,5-million for the 1979/80 financial year. Between 1978 and 1980 South African grants amounted to approximately R573-million.

Corruption in the homeland drastically depleted its funds and in 1980 the South African state assumed control over the homeland's budget.

When the Minister of Education, Stella Sigcau, was fired in 1979, a cabinet crisis ensued, and the opposition Progressive Democratic Party (DPP) was formed under the leadership of Dalindyebo, Matanzima's old rival. But Matanzima used his 'state powers' against his opponent. Trumped-up charges against Dalindyebo saw him convicted on a minor charge, but he was acquitted of the more serious charges. There was much public support for Dalindyebo, and the Transkei administration suffered great embarrassment.

In 1980 most of the members of the opposition DPP were arrested, and some were banned. Dalindyebo fled and went into exile in Zambia, where he forged links with the ANC. He died in 1986.

However Matanzima's TNIP was also rocked by splits and divisions during 1979 and 1980. The party lost support in East Pondoland when the powerful Sigcau clan switched sides and allied with the DPP. Matanzima decided to appoint his brother George as Prime Minister, while he assumed the position of President.

George Matanzima's brutal attempts to centralise control resulted in a further disintegration of the tribal alliances his brother had painstakingly constructed. The entire ruling apparatus was wracked by crises. Heavy repressive measures saw many opposition leaders, former cabinet ministers and the head of the defence force and police detained. The former Rhodesian Selous Scout General Ron Reid-Daly was appointed head of the Transkei Defence Force.

In 1985, Apartheid practitioners conceived a plan to merge the Transkei and Ciskei and create a 'united nation of Xhosa speakers' who they thought would support the South African government and help it to stamp out unrest in the Eastern Cape. Matanzima had long held ambitions to rule such a territory, and had opposed the 'independence' of Ciskei in 1981 in the hope that this merger would be realised. But the plan, which included having Ciskei's president, Lennox Sebe, assassinated, failed after it was leaked to General Bantu Holomisa.

Matanzima began to lose support by the mid-1980s, and resigned in 1986, but he managed to retain his seat as Paramount Chief of Western Tembuland. He was succeeded as President by Paramount Chief Tutor Ngangelizwe Ndamase, the son of Chief Victor Poto of Western Pondoland. George Matanzima, who had been embroiled in disputes with his brother, was effectively sidelined, but the conflicts intensified and brought much turbulence to Transkeian politics in the period from 1986 to 1989.

Eventually, both Chief Victor Poto and George Matanzima were overthrown, amid charges of corruption in government departments. Others also lost their positions, including Reid-Daly, the head of the Transkeian Defence Force. He was replaced by General Zondwa Mtirara in April 1987.

With the army in crisis, George Matanzima fled the country in October 1987, but was subsequently apprehended and charged with misappropriation of funds. The TNIP chose Stella Sigcau to replace him as Prime Minister, but she was ousted when General Bantu Holomisa mounted a bloodless coup in January 1988. Holomisa ruled as chairperson of the Military Council.

Earlier, in April 1986, the son of the deceased Sabata Dalindyebo, Buyelekhaya, brought his father's body back to the Transkei to be buried at the Great Place. Matanzima had the body seized and buried in a pauper's grave. But Holomisa supported Buyelekhaya, encouraging him to return and take up his father's position as Paramount Chief of Thembuland. With the support of the Congress of traditional Leaders (Contralesa), Buyelekhaya returned in October 1989, and reburied his father's body in a public ceremony. Members of ANC-aligned anti-apartheid groupings, together with King Mswati II of Swaziland, were among those who attended the ceremony.

In the meanwhile, Holomisa took the step to unban the UDF and other anti-apartheid organisations in Transkeian territory, a move that could not be opposed by the newly inaugurated President of South Africa, F.W. de Klerk. Holomisa also announced that he would conduct a plebiscite to test whether Transkeians wanted their homeland to be reincorporated into South Africa.

All these events played out against a backdrop of economic failure and corruption. The homeland's leaders had never managed to develop an autonomous economy. Despite incentives to industrialists, Matanzima failed to persuade foreign firms to set up industrial plants in his territory. Only one bag factory was established in the early 1980s, and in the enterprises that were established, Transkeians were exploited in the workplace.

Most of the employed worked for the bureaucracy. A small consumer goods industry employed a total of 4050 people in 1975. Of the total of 47,000 waged workers in the Transkei in 1975, more than 20,000 were employees of the 'state'. More than 500,000 Transkeians were working in South Africa, remitting money to their families. These remittances made up 70% of the homeland's total GNP.

Like Bophuthatswana's Lucas Mangope, who secured lucrative deals with Hoteliers and casino owners such as Sol Kerzner, George Matanzima demanded and received R2-million from Kerzner so the latter could set up a gambling monopoly in the homeland.

A Commission of Enquiry appointed after George Matanzima fled the country established that between 1976 and 1988, R200-million had been misappropriated by the Matanzimas.

In November 1990, a group of six white and black soldiers attempted to mount a coup, but they failed when troops loyal to Holomisa overcame the plotters. Eighteen people were killed, including the leader of the coup, Colonel Craig Duli.

Under the new democratic dispensation in South Africa, the Transkei and all other homelands were incorporated into South Africa in 1994.

Ciskei

The Ciskei homeland is established
Thursday, 14 November 1968
The Ciskei was established under the Bantu Authorities Act of 1951 as an 'independent republic'. The creation of Ciskei was in line with apartheid policies of the South African government. The Ciskei and the Transkei were two designated "states" for the Xhosa speaking people in the Eastern Cape. In 1981 it was granted "independence" under the presidency of Lennox Sebe. In March 1990, Sebe was toppled by the military and replaced by Brigadier Joshua Oupa Gqozo.

After South Africa's first democratic elections Ciskei was re-incorporated into South Africa.

Bophuthatswana

Bophuthatswana is granted independence by the South African government
Tuesday, 6 December 1977

Thirty-four years ago, on 6 December 1977, Bophuthatswana was granted 'independence' by the South African government. The region became the second Bantustan to gain 'independence' following the Transkei, a year earlier. The region's President, Lucas Mangope, launched a campaign to construct top-class facilities, including hospitals, schools and sports grounds.

After the 1994 elections, Bophuthatswana, together with other homelands, was incorporated to form part of South Africa's nine provinces. It is now part of the North West Province. Other parts of the homeland have been incorporated into the Northern Cape Province.

Before 1994 a pro ANC faction in the homeland, led by Malebane Metsing, unsuccessfully attempted to oust Mangope. But it had become apparent that the end for the homeland government and their apartheid overlords was imminent. A group of Afrikaner right-wingers, in a bid to keep Mangope at the helm, entered the homeland. They hoped to prevent the homeland falling under the influence of the ANC or any of the political formations opposed to apartheid. The army and police dealt with the intruders, leaving scores of people dead.

Kwazulu Natal

Old Natal Province and the old homeland KwaZulu coats of arms

The homeland of KwaZulu (or place of the Zulu) was granted self-government under apartheid on 1 December 1977. According to the apartheid social planner's ideal of 'separate development', it was intended to be the home of the Zulu people. Although it was relatively large, it was segmented and spread over a large area in what is now the province of KwaZulu-Natal.

The capital of KwaZulu was Ulundi and its government was led by Chief Magosuthu Buthelezi, leader of the Inkatha Freedom Party (IFP), who established a good relationship with the ruling National Party. He also distanced himself from the African National Congress (ANC), with whom he had a close relationship.

The government offered Buthelezi and KwaZulu the status of fully 'independent homeland' several times during the 1980s. He continually refused, saying he wanted the approximately 4 million residents of the homeland to remain South African citizens. Nonetheless, Buthelezi claimed chief ministerial privileges and powers in the area. In 1994, KwaZulu became a part of South Africa when it merged with the former Natal to become KwaZulu-Natal.

KwaZulu-Natal was made up of the old province of Natal, and the old homeland of KwaZulu. It also has a Zulu king, Goodwill Zwelithini, based in Ulundi. He has some representative power for the Zulu people, but only under the government of South Africa. Pietermaritzburg is now the capital city, and the main languages in KwaZulu Natal are Zulu, English and Afrikaans.

Frank Mdlalose of Inkatha Freedom Party (IFP) was the first Premier of KwaZulu Natal in 1994, and his successor was Ben Ngubane of IFP in 1997. Lionel Mtshali of IFP took became the Premier in 1999, the last year of IFP's governing of KwaZulu Natal province. In 2004, African National Congress (ANC) took over and S'bu Ndebele became the Premier, and his successor was Zweli Mkhize of ANC in 2009, followed by Senzo Mchunu of ANC in 2013. In 2014, Senzo Mchunu was given another term as the Premier of KwaZulu Natal.

The Drankesberg is situated in KwaZulu-Natal. The Zulu call the Drakensberg-range uKhahlamba, because it looks like a row of spears. There are many superstitious stories about spirits and monsters in the Berg (as it is called). In 1877, a newspaper in Bloemfontein wrote about a farmer and his son who said that they had seen a dragon fly over the mountains.

The Berg plays an important role in South Africa's history and heritage. It was the home of the Zulu kingdom and the birthplace of many of its Kings. During the Great Trek many Afrikaners had to cross these mountains with their ox-wagons. Many battles were fought here, between Shaka's Zulus and other groups, between the Zulu and the British in the Anglo-Zulu War, and between the British and the Boers in the Anglo-Boer War.

There are also many San rock paintings in the mountains, some of them are 8000 years old. Today, the uKhahlamba Drakensberg Park is a World Heritage Site.

There are many battle sites in KwaZulu-Natal. These battle sites include the Battle of Blood River or (Ncome River), where a life-size model of the Voortrekker laager can be seen exactly where it stood over 100 years ago. There are also many battle sites from the Anglo-Zulu War and Anglo-Boer War with monuments or museums that tell the stories of the sites. The homeland of KwaZulu (or place of the Zulu) was granted self-government under apartheid on 1 December 1977. According to the apartheid social planner's ideal of 'separate development', it was intended to be the home of the Zulu people. Although it was relatively large, it was segmented and spread over a large area in what is now the province of KwaZulu-Natal.

The capital of KwaZulu was Ulundi and its government was led by Chief Magosuthu Buthelezi, leader of the Inkatha Freedom Party (IFP), who established a good relationship with the ruling National Party. He also distanced himself from the African National Congress (ANC), with whom he had a close relationship.

The government offered Buthelezi and KwaZulu the status of fully 'independent homeland' several times during the 1980s. He continually refused, saying he wanted the approximately 4 million residents of the homeland to remain South African citizens. Nonetheless, Buthelezi claimed chief ministerial privileges and powers in the area. In 1994, KwaZulu became a part of South Africa when it merged with the former Natal to become KwaZulu-Natal.

KwaZulu-Natal was made up of the old province of Natal, and the old homeland of KwaZulu. It also has a Zulu king, Goodwill Zwelithini, based in Ulundi. He has some representative power for the Zulu people, but only under the government of South Africa. Pietermaritzburg is now the capital city, and the main languages in KwaZulu Natal are Zulu, English and Afrikaans.

Frank Mdlalose of Inkatha Freedom Party (IFP) was the first Premier of KwaZulu Natal in 1994, and his successor was Ben Ngubane of IFP in 1997. Lionel Mtshali of IFP took became the Premier in 1999, the last year of IFP's governing of KwaZulu Natal province. In 2004, African National Congress (ANC) took over and S'bu Ndebele became the Premier, and his successor was Zweli Mkhize of ANC in 2009, followed by Senzo Mchunu of ANC in 2013. In 2014, Senzo Mchunu was given another term as the Premier of KwaZulu Natal.

The Drankesberg is situated in KwaZulu-Natal. The Zulu call the Drakensberg-range uKhahlamba, because it looks like a row of spears. There are many superstitious stories about spirits and monsters in the Berg (as it is called). In 1877, a newspaper in Bloemfontein wrote about a farmer and his son who said that they had seen a dragon fly over the mountains.

The Berg plays an important role in South Africa's history and heritage. It was the home of the Zulu kingdom and the birthplace of many of its Kings. During the Great Trek many Afrikaners had to cross these mountains with their ox-wagons. Many battles were fought here, between Shaka's Zulus and other groups, between the Zulu and the British in the Anglo-Zulu War, and between the British and the Boers in the Anglo-Boer War.

There are also many San rock paintings in the mountains, some of them are 8000 years old. Today, the uKhahlamba Drakensberg Park is a World Heritage Site.

There are many battle sites in KwaZulu-Natal. These battle sites include the Battle of Blood River or (Ncome River), where a life-size model of the Voortrekker laager can be seen exactly where it stood over 100 years ago. There are also many battle sites from the Anglo-Zulu War and Anglo-Boer War with monuments or museums that tell the stories of the sites.

Lebowa

During the apartheid period, Lebowa was the homeland of the North Sotho people. It became a semi-independent national state in 1972. The territory was fragmented into six separate areas scattered throughout the northern Transvaal. Seshego and Lebowakgomo, the capital, were the main growth points. The Chief Minister during most of the 1980s was Dr C N M Phatudi. In 1994, it was reincorporated into South Africa and it became part of the Limpopo Province.

KaNgwane

The South African government is to grant self-government to KaNgwane

The South African government was to grant self-government to KaNgwane. This move was seen as confirmation that it had finally abandoned its land deal with Swaziland, of which KaNgwane was to have been part. South Africa and Swaziland were not new to conflicting claims about land. In September 1982, the Appeal Court in Bloemfontein ruled that the Presidential Proclamation issued in June

1982, claiming to restore Ingwavuma, in then-named Natal, to South African jurisdiction, was null and void since the State President had acted improperly.

The territory in question was formally designated in 1977 with the name of AmaSwazi, and its destination was to be transferred to Swaziland. Later, this attempt failed after popular protests in 1982 and was dissolved. Two years later, the homeland was recreated and renamed KaNgwane. Subsequently, it was announced that a Commission under the chairmanship of Judge Frans Rumpff, would be appointed to investigate and report on conflicting claims between KwaZulu and Swaziland.

QwaQwa

The QwaQwa homeland receives self-government status
Friday, 1 November 1974
Qwaqwa was one of the ten homelands in South Africa introduced by the apartheid government. It was home to the Batlokoa and Bakwena Southern Sotho sub-tribes. The word Qwaqwa hails from the San language meaning 'whiter than white' which was in reference to the sandstone that makes up most of the homeland's rocky Drakensberg mountain.

From 1974, the homeland became a self-governing state under the leadership of Kenneth Mopeli until 1994 when South Africa became a democracy. It was then dissolved to form part of the Free State Province. All the other nine independent and dependant homelands were also dissolved.

Gazankulu

Gazankulu was the homeland of the Shangaan and Tsonga people in South Africa. It was divided over two territories, west of the Kruger National Park, and its capital was at Giyani. It did not accept independence from South Africa, but was granted self-government in 1973. However, like the other nine homelands, the rest of the world did not accept it as a state. Since 1994, the former homeland of Gazankulu has formed part of the Limpopo Province.

Joshua Berry

Traditional leaders Responsibilities during Apartheid period

The institution of traditional leadership represents an early form of societal organisation. It embodies the protection of culture, traditions, customs and values. During the pre-colonial era, the institution of traditional leadership was a political and administrative centre of governance for traditional rural communities in South Africa. The institution of traditional leadership was the form of government with the highest authority. The leadership control of traditional leaders changed when the colonial authority and rulers introduced their authority to the landscape of traditional governance.

In the pre-colonial era, 1880 -1893, traditional authorities were important institutions which guided the traditional life. Traditional leaders played an important role in the everyday administration of their areas and the lives of traditional people. Traditional authorities provided political, societal, economic, cultural and religious leadership for local communities. The relationship between the traditional community and traditional leader was very important and highly respected. The normal functioning and existence of each traditional community was the responsibility of the traditional leader. Traditional leaders were not elected, but the son would inherit the father or uncle's leadership position. Traditional leadership was based on the principle of governance of the people, where a traditional leader was accountable to his people. The Black South African population was organised into group with a centralised leadership vested in hereditary leaders called Chiefs.

During the colonial period, the 19th century, traditional authorities were the means of indirect rule. Indirect rule was established to administer Africans under the colonial administration rather than give them the right to vote. Indirect rule was a British concept where traditional leaders became agents of the colonial government. These leaders depended on the colonial government for resources and power. Thus the traditional leaders were given orders by the colonial government as to how to administer and control their communities.

The policy of indirect rule appeared falsely to protect the pre-colonial structures of the traditional leadership. In practice, it was established as a means of controlling traditional communities in their ethnic areas.

The pre-colonial leadership's domination of traditional leaders changed when the colonial rulers introduced their authorities. Through the colonial system, traditional leaders were obliged to work for the colonial government constituted by the British. The traditional authorities were acknowledged and given form by the colonial government to suit, adopt and promote the objectives and aims of its colonial strategies and missions. The aims and objectives of the colonial government were: to control the economic, political and social system, as well as maintain White domination.

The traditional leaders roles included: judicial functions, allocation of land held in trust (the ownership of the land is hold by the traditional leader for the benefits of the people who live in it), the preservation of law and order, the provision of administrative services at local government, administration of social welfare such as the processing of applications for social security benefits and businesses, premises, the promotion of education such as the erection and maintenance of schools and the administration of access to education and finance.

In order to change pre-colonial powers, roles and structures of traditional leadership, and ensure that traditional authorities promote the colonial government's strategies and objectives, the colonial government of South Africa passed Black Administration Act of 1927.

The Act was passed to restrict the powers and roles of traditional leaders. The Black Administration Act of 1951 was passed to control the traditional authorities and traditional courts. At the same time, the Act aimed at the recognition and application of customary law in order to control the institution of traditional leadership by making sure that Blacks were subjected to a political regime from the remainder of the country. Black Authorities Act of 1951 was also passed to give traditional leaders the powers to control the land at regional, tribal and territorial levels.

The office of Governor-General was created with the aim of prescribing traditional leaders' duties and autonomy. The Governor-General had the powers to appoint whosoever was considered by the government to be a Chief, irrespective of whether such a person was entitled to the position by the natural and traditional laws of succession. The Governor-General was also empowered to remove and replace any traditional leader who was not willing to implement the colonial government's policies. This was due to the fact that the Governor-General was made the Supreme Chief of all traditional leaders in the then Union of South Africa.

In 1948, the National Party under the leadership of DF Malan came to power. The traditional leadership system fitted its plan of separate development. In 1951, the Bantu Authorities Act was passed, making traditional leaders the administrative agents of the Apartheid state in the reserve areas, starting a process of setting up new separate political institutions for the African population. This was reinforced by the passing of the Promotion of Bantu Self-Government Act in 1959, which provided for the establishment of 10 self-governing homelands or Bantustans. The Homelands were areas whereby Africans, who were denied South African citizenship, could exercise citizenship rights within a territorial authority where an ethnically defined administrative system was based on tribal authority.

The colonial and Apartheid government also took away certain rights such as control over the distribution and administration of land. That resulted in a fundamental change in the leadership roles of the traditional leaders. Bantustans such as Transkei, Bophuthatswana, Venda and Ciskei provided a good example of change in the leadership roles of the traditional leaders during the colonial period. Traditional authorities colluded in the segregationist policies of the South African government.

South African Race and Tribes, their Roots

Afrikaner

From European to "African land"

The modern Afrikaner is descended mainly from Western Europeans who settled on the southern tip of Africa during the middle of the 17th century. Portuguese mariners discovered the sea passage to the East round Cape Point in 1488 and in the course of their visits, came into contact with the Khoi. Initially cultural differences caused conflict and the Portuguese conveyed a biased image of a 'hostile' Africa to the Western world.

Nevertheless, for the commercially active Dutch the Cape was the ideal halfway station on the sea route to the East, and the Dutch East India Company (VOC) established a refreshment post in Table Bay (present day Cape Town). In 1657 officials (mostly Dutch and Germans) could retire from the Company's service and become Free

Burghers (independent farmers). In 1688 a group of French Protestants, striving for religious freedom, fled from France and settled in the Cape. Together with the Free Burghers they are regarded as the earliest ancestors of the Afrikaner nation.

According to J.A. Heese and C. Pama, by 1867 the 'Afrikaners' constituted a mixture of:

Dutch (34, 8%)

Germans (33, 7%)

French (13, 2%)

People of colour (7%)

British (5, 2%)

Unknown origin (3, 5%)

Other Europeans (2, 6%)

A unique cultural group was formed which identified itself completely with African soil. As early as 1707, Hendrik Biebouw (Bibault) referred to himself as an "Africaander". This community developed their own language, national identity, history and religion. They differed radically from the indigenous Khoi and San and also from the south-moving Bantu-speaking peoples whom they would later encounter deeper into the interior.

In 2006, a census determined that just over 5 million South Africans speak Afrikaans as their home language. Afrikaans is also spoken in the Republic of Namibia, and by South Africans living and working in the United Kingdom, USA, Canada, Australia and New Zealand.

Language, Culture and Beliefs

Religion: The Afrikaner's Religious Experience

Afrikaner religion stems from the Protestant practices of the 17th century Reformed Church of Holland. Other religious influences in South Africa came from British English-speaking ministers in the early 1800s, and the Swiss reformer John Calvin (1509–1564) who was brought to South Africa by French settlers. Calvin believed the church should influence government policy, and that races should remain pure and separate. All these influences led to the development of a unique brand of Protestantism in South Africa. Government policies on apartheid (separate development of races) were supported by Afrikaner religious doctrines.

The Dutch and French who settled in the Cape were committed Calvinists or Reformed Protestants. Anyone who accepted the Christian faith was accepted in the Western cultural community. Those outside were regarded as heathens while the Eastern slaves were predominantly Muslim.

By 1795, there were seven Dutch Reformed congregations in the Cape, and Calvinism became the foundation of the Afrikaner's philosophy of life and view of the world. It also influenced all aspects of his cultural activities. In addition, individuality and independence were intensified by a pioneering existence. The migrant farmers and pioneers who took part in the Great Trek into the interior didn't have any kind of organized church life and not having ministers of religion, their only source of knowledge was the bible. In their struggle for survival they gradually came to identify themselves with the nation of Israel.

With the establishment of another two Dutch Reformed (Hervormde and Gereformeerde) churches in the 1850s in the Transvaal three so-called sister churches originated. Afrikaners believed that they were called to spread the Christian faith in Africa. The influence of their Christian-national beliefs figured strongly in government and schools.

Festivals

Festivals are part of the Afrikaner's existence and fill a need to express joy or humility over certain events. New Year and the so-called Dingaan's Day or Day of the Covenant memorial festivals were traditionally celebrated annually even before the South African War (Anglo-Boer War).

The centenary of the Great Trek in 1938 was the inspiration for a people's festival. People all over the country became involved and celebrations were organized even in the smallest villages. The highlight was on a hill outside Pretoria where thousands of people gathered for the laying of the corner stone of the Voortrekker Monument on the 16th of December. In 1949 a second festival was held during the inauguration of the Monument (13-16 December).

Several other centenaries were celebrated with much pomp and circumstance such as the arrival of Jan van Riebeeck (1652) in 1952. Political events were celebrated with festivals such as the Union Festival in 1960 and the Republic Festival in 1966 when the Republic of South Africa (RSA) was five years old. Cities and towns usually celebrate their own centenaries with local festivities.

In addition, some organizations arrange festivals on a smaller scale to commemorate certain events. Regional celebrations such as the Biltong Festival in Somerset-East or the Mampoer (traditional liquor distilled from fruit) Festival at the Willem Prinsloo Agricultural Museum, Pretoria, is held annually. The 1990s saw the start of annual arts festivals - the Klein Karoo National Arts Festival (Oudtshoorn) followed by Aardklop in Potchefstroom, InniBos in Nelspruit and many others.

Afrikaners also continue to celebrate their heritage in traditional ways and on special occasions don traditional dress and take part in formal dancing called volkspele. On these occasions, boys and men wear shorts with knee socks, and women wear long dresses and bonnets. Male folk dancing partners also wear shirts with vests and long pants.

Music

Afrikaners are particularly fond of music and song. During the Great Trek and in the early pioneering days this was expressed in the singing of religious songs. Light music was made using instruments such as the violin, and the concertina and would later develop into a traditional Afrikaans music form, namely 'Boeremusiek'.

Afrikaners only really began to compose Afrikaans music after the TweedeTaalbeweging (Second Language Movement) c. 1905 when poets were able to express themselves in Afrikaans and the poems were set to music. J.H.G. Bosman did pioneering work with the music he composed for Eugene Marais' 'Winternag' in 1908. This was the beginning of the Afrikaans art song. Composers who made significant contributions before 1930 were S. le Roux Marais, Stephen Eyssen, and M.L. de Villiers. After 1930 musicians such as Gideon Fagan, Arnold van Wyk, Hubert du Plessis and Stefans Grove played important roles.

After 1945, a few operas were translated into Afrikaans and performed, but opera was to remain a foreign art form for most Afrikaans speakers. Afrikaans opera singers did, however, make their mark. Cecilia Wessels became famous abroad for her roles in operas. Mimi Coertse will be remembered for her wonderful contribution to music - in Afrikaans, but also for all the years she performed in opera houses abroad.

It is in the field of popular music that Afrikaners made an enormous contribution - Jannie du Toit, Koos du Plessis, Laurika Rauch, and several other artists would become famous. The Musiek- en Liriekbeweging (Music and Lyrics Movement) heralds the beginning of a new era of modern, original Afrikaans music.

In the 1980s, musicians protested against the government of the day. This culminated in the Voelvry Movement which built up a big following amongst the youth as they toured to and performed on university campuses.

Since the 1990s and particularly since arts festivals became popular, there has been renewed interest in and support for Afrikaans music amongst the youth. Afrikaans artists produce popular as well as alternative music and have caused an explosion in Afrikaans music sales.

Fine Arts

By the end of the nineteenth century, a number of Dutch artists such as Frans Oerder had settled in South Africa and overtime became Afrikaners. Oerder took part in the Anglo-Boer War as an official war artist on the side of the Boers. As early as 1898, Anton van Wouw had started work on the statue of Paul Kruger which today graces Church Square in Pretoria. These artists were exponents of Realism, which was popular amongst their compatriots, and they became teachers of a new generation.

Van Wouw also created several excellent bronze statues and is, par excellence, the great Afrikaans sculptor of the people. Coert Steynberg will also be remembered for his many statues and monuments. Afrikaans sculptors produced a large number of national monuments and statues of Afrikaner heroes.

J.E.A. Volschenk was the first Afrikaner to become a professional painter. He particularly captured South African landscapes on canvas. W.H. Coetzer's interest in Afrikaner history resulted in the creation of several historical paintings.

Erich Mayer loved South Africa, its landscapes and its people. He was a pioneer in developing Afrikaans art, and his work is of great cultural historical value. J.H. Pierneef developed a style of his own which could only have originated in South Africa-a new way of portraying nature. His lino cuts and etches eternalized many historical buildings. Maggie Laubser also developed her own definitive style.

In addition, Afrikaans artists made significant contributions to other fields of art such as stained glass, ceramics, mixed media and mosaics.

Literature

After the South African War the Tweede Afrikaanse Taalbeweging (Second Afrikaans Language Movement) developed, which would build upon the foundation laid in the nineteenth century. Eugene Marais' striking poem 'Winternag' was published as early as 1905 and in 1915, Totius became the first recipient of the Hertzog Prize for Literature.

In 1914, Afrikaans was recognized by the Cape Provincial Council and in 1925 was acknowledged by the legislator as an official language. Gradually scientific works began to be published in Afrikaans, facilitated by the first edition of the Afrikaanse Woordelys en Spelreels (Afrikaans Word List and Spelling Rules) in 1917. The highlight for most Afrikaners was the launch of the Afrikaans Bible in 1933.

Initially, few women ventured to write, but in 1936 Elisabeth Eybers made her debut as the first female poet in Afrikaans.

Afrikaans authors and poets contributed to every genre and in the 1960s protest literature was published, criticising the government of the day and its policies. In terms of the power vested in the Publication Board in 1963, some lyrics, films, and publications which threatened public morals or safety, were banned.

Publications in the form of newspapers and magazines date back to the second decade of the 20th century. The first Die Huisgenoot appeared in 1916, and Die Landbouweekblad in 1919. These prepared the way for other family publications while a number of organizations like the ATKV and the FAK began to launch their own publications.

The wealth of literature that still appears in Afrikaans proves that the language is alive and well.

Sport

On an international level, Afrikaners excelled in individual sports such as boxing and wrestling soon after the Anglo-Boer War, and later in athletics. But it would be rugby that found favour at an early stage. Afrikaners contributed on all levels to South Africans becoming renowned as one of the greatest rugby nations in the world, and the world champions in 1995 and 2007.

Various illustrious individuals, like Danie Craven, Mannetjies Roux, Frik du Preez, Dawie de Villiers and Naas Botha and families such as the

Morkels, Du Plessis' and Burger-families, as well as rugby-commentator Gerhard Viviers and many others became part of popular Afrikaner culture.

Success or failure on the rugby field has a direct impact on the morale and attitude of most Afrikaners. On the other hand Afrikaners, unlike their fellow citizens, are still relatively uninvolved in soccer. Since the Afrikaners are an especially sporting nation, it was used as an effective weapon against the South African government in the years of conflict and international isolation.

After South Africa was readmitted to international sport, Afrikaners also made a difference on the cricket field. Golfers like Ernie Els, Retief Goosen and Trevor Immelman currently excel on the golf course whilst swimmers such as Ryk Neethling and Roland Schoeman shatter various world records.

Architecture

Afrikaans architecture is associated with an intrinsic architectural style that began with the construction of Cape Town by the Dutch in the late 17th century. Monumental public buildings, houses of commerce, private dwellings, churches and rural estates of that period reflect the ornamented, but severe style of colonial Dutch architecture, which was influenced by traditions from the Dutch East Indies.

Even in the smallest towns, Afrikaans Dutch Reformed churches contributed to an important architectural aspect to the country, with their soaring steeples and classic stonework.

Origins

Afrikaans/ Afrikaners in the Cape

The Afrikaans dialect spoken today originates from the Dutch language spoken by early settlers in the 1600s. However, modern Afrikaans is in fact an accumulation of many other influences, which include other languages, both foreign and indigenous.

The influence of other languages on the development of the Afrikaans dialect began after 1652, when sailors who had been shipwrecked off the Cape coast incorporated terms and phrases into the dialect. This influence was significant, as many ships passed through the Cape after a trade route via the horn of Africa became viable. These phrases, both English and Portuguese in origin, soon found their way into the then predominantly Dutch dialect.

At this stage, before Afrikaans became an established and written language, it was referred to as Cape Dutch or Kitchen Dutch. This is because it acted mainly as a spoken language for people living in the Cape, with Dutch used as the formal and written language. The first known example of written Afrikaans appeared in a poem dated 7 August 1795, written about the Battle of Muizenberg. Other early work in Afrikaans included the use of the Arabic alphabet, for example in the work Bayaan-ud-djyn written by Abu Bakr in the mid 1800s.

The Afrikaans dialect took on a different flavour with the arrival of slaves in the Cape. Naturally, they all spoke different African and Asian languages, depending on their origins. Slaves from India and the East Indies for example, spoke a mixture of Indian and Indonesian languages. All these languages, accents, dialects and phrases, along with Khoikhoi dialects, began to influence the way people communicated on the farms. Mixed with Dutch and German, the result became a dialect known as Afrikaans. This dialect was further developed by Huguenot settlers, who contributed different words to the Afrikaans vocabulary, and altered the sounds of certain words.

These Huguenots, along with other Free Burghers, had been granted rights to land by the VOC management (1652-1795), and began farming to generate income. In the area of the Cape Peninsula, where they had limited access to education and cultural opportunities, these Free Burghers soon established grain and wine farms, which thrived due to favourable economic conditions.

In order to maintain these farms, slaves were imported for manual labour from the East. According to records, by 1170 there were 8104 slaves versus 7949 burghers with their families in the Cape. As these slaves were also employed as domestic servants, aspects of Eastern culture such as music, food dishes and words became an intrinsic part of the developing Afrikaner culture.

The movement of Afrikaners into the interior

Cattle farmers, also known as itinerant ('trek') farmers, or trek boers, stayed on the move in search of pasture. Eventually, by the end of the 18th century many of them lived in isolation, some as far as 1 000 km from Cape Town. As a result of their constant battle for survival against nature and the indigenous peoples, theirs was a struggling existence with few opportunities to develop culturally. Travellers often referred to their 'backwardness' which was in sharp contrast with the almost flamboyant life style of many 'Afrikaners' (farmers and officials) in the Cape.

The consequences of British colonisation of the Cape after 1806 (i.e. conflict with the Xhosa as a result of the Eastern border and the anglicizing policies, and the manner in which the British freed the slaves) fired the Afrikaners' craving for independence and this led to the Great Trek (1836-1854) into the interior. In spite of inadequate training and political know-how, the sheer willpower of these pioneers resulted in the establishment in 1852 of the South African Republic (ZAR) and of the Republic of the Orange Free State (OVS) in 1854. These republics became known as the Boer republics and the inhabitants would be internationally known as the "Boers'.

The determination and courage of these pioneers became the single most important element in the folk memory of Afrikaner Nationalism, and significant developments in the consolidation of the Afrikaans language and culture began with the "Groot Trek".

Around this time, three main Afrikaans dialects had emerged, Cape Afrikaans, Orange River Afrikaans and Eastern Border Afrikaans. The Cape dialect remains infused with the language spoken by Malay slaves who worked in the Cape, and spoke a form of broken Portuguese. The Orange River dialect developed with the influence of Khoi languages and dialects developed in the Namaqualand and Griqualand West regions, and the Eastern Border Afrikaans evolved from the settlers who moved east towards Natal from the Cape.

The move towards Afrikaans as an official language

Die Genootskap van Regte Afrikaners (GRA), an organization that promoted the Afrikaans language, was formed by Rev. S.J. Du Toit on 14 August 1875. By this time, the language was spoken by many people of different races and ethnic groups throughout Southern Africa. As the language evolved further, White Afrikaans speakers distanced themselves from the English-speaking community, due to resentment after their defeat in the South African War of 1899- 1902.

This resentment was exacerbated by the treatment of Afrikaans women and children in war concentration camps, the British "scorched earth policy" and resulting Afrikaner destitution. The loss of Afrikaner morale prompted a 'Kultuur' [culture] campaign to promote the Afrikaans language, and lead to the establishment of the Afrikaner Broederbond (Brotherhood). The Broederbond in turn established other cultural institutions such as FAK (Federasie van Afrikaanse Kultuurvereniginge). In 1924, Afrikaans, as opposed to Dutch, was given official recognition, and a new South African flag was introduced three years later.

The National Party was also instrumental in the consolidation of Afrikaner culture, as it emphasized Afrikaner Nationalism and racial separation. Therefore, when the party won the South African elections of 1948, measures were introduced to give preference to White Afrikaans speakers in terms of employment and business. The National Party's institution of apartheid was overtly criticized, and was vehemently protested against. A significant example of anti-apartheid protest was the Soweto Uprising of 1976, when Afrikaans was declared the sole medium of instruction in so called "Bantu" schools.

Unfortunately, the National Party's ruthless apartheid regime and simultaneous promotion of the language continues to associate the language with an oppressive political system. During apartheid, Afrikaans was 1 of only 2 official languages. However, today it is one of 11 official South African languages recognized by the Constitution.

Related Languages

Fanagalo

Afrikaans has also formed part of pidgin languages such as Fanagalo (or Fanakalo), which was developed in order to create a common language on the mines, which employed workers from a variety of cultural and linguistic backgrounds. Fanagalo has elements of the Nguni languages, English and Afrikaans.

Afrikaans, which was first spoken in the Cape Colony, was also originally a pidgin language, or a language that has been grammatically simplified from a parent language, with the addition of local language elements.

Like Fanagalo, Afrikaans was also developed so that people who did not share a common language could communicate with each other.

Gamtaal

Gamtaal is a dialect of Afrikaans spoken on the Cape Flats, a district of Cape Town. The name derives from the term gammat taal, the word gammat a derogatory word to describe a 'young malay' or 'young coloured'.

According to Adam Haupt, gamtaal is seen as an 'authentic' language representative of the Coloured working class, and has been used in the songs of musicians such as Prophets of the City (POC) and Brasse van die Kaap (BVK).

Sotho (South Sotho or Basotho)

Sotho (South Sotho or Basotho) people are concentrated in the Free State, Gauteng and Eastern Cape Provinces, with small groups in Namibia and Zambia. While the Sotho people's history is not directly intertwined with that of Bloemfontein, their history had an important influence on the history and development of the Orange Free State province.

Origins:

The four major ethnic divisions among Black South Africans are the Nguni, Sotho-Tswana, Shangaan-Tsonga and Venda. Together the Nguni and Sotho account for the largest percentage of the total Black population. The major Sotho groups are the South Sotho (Basuto and Sotho), the West Sotho (Tswana), and the North Sotho (Pedi).

Early Sotho origins and history is largely unknown, but Ironworkers, who were probably Sotho-speakers, were at Phalaborwa from the eighth century and at Melville Koppies in the Johannesburg area from the eleventh century. Oral tradition has it that the founding lineage knew the art of smelting and ancient ritual dances are associated with it.

Archaeologists have produced indisputable evidence of Sotho-speaking people smelting at widely dispersed places in Gauteng, the North West Province, the Northern Province, and Botswana. The first pottery in South Africa associated with the Sotho is called Icon and dates to between 1300 and 1500. As with the Nguni, anthropological and linguistic data suggest an East African origin for Sotho-Tswana speakers, in this case in what is now Tanzania.

By 1500 the Sotho groups had expanded to the south and west and separated into the three distinct clusters; the South Sotho (later became the Basuto and Sotho), the West Sotho (later the Tswana), and the North Sotho (later the Pedi). It is important to note however that all three clusters share very similar dialects, beliefs and social structures and the main distinctions between the three groups were only established as a result of the early 19th century difiqane period.

Most Sotho people were herders of cattle, goats, and sheep, and cultivators of grains and tobacco. In addition, the Sotho people were skilled craftsmen, renowned for their metalworking, leatherworking, and wood and ivory carving. In fact, most archaeologists presume the Sotho were the main body of early stone builders in this part of the country, because Iron Age sites studied by them resemble the areas reported by early eyewitnesses very closely.

The South Sotho cluster is associated with the Fokeng, who are today Sotho-speaking. They were long believed to be the first Sotho speakers on the highveld and have always been respected by oral historians as the most ancient of the Sotho peoples. Recent archaeological research has suggested, however, that the Fokeng were originally Nguni in culture and dispersed from Ntsuanatsatsi near Frankfort in the present Free State. They reached the edges of the Caledon valley in the 1600s, where the Phetla had already settled. North of the Vaal they made contact with Southwestern and then Western Sotho-Tswana folk.

In the Waterberg in the 1600s, conflict over limited resources seems to have provoked discord, in this case between Nguni speakers and mixed groups of Fokeng and Western Sotho-Tswana people. Sometime before 1700, some Western Sotho-Tswana people, including Kwena communities, moved south across the Vaal, into the Fokeng area. As a result of this contact and acculturation, the Fokeng became Sotho and, in the Free State, all but vanished.

In turn, Western and Southwestern groups in the 1700s adopted building in stone from the Fokeng. People of each cluster built distinctive stonewalled settlements, which presumably reflected the details of their earlier settlements of wood and thatch. The variously organised settlements, like ceramics, allow archaeologists to trace movement and interaction across the landscape. What is clear is that pulses of settlement shifts and conflict seem to have been at least partly a response to climatic flux during the Little Ice Age. For instance, an improved climate after 1700 made it possible for Southwestern Sotho-Tswana to settle south of the Vaal River, on the western edges of Fokeng-Kwena territory.

From 1750 onwards, intensifying trade and more intrusive colonial expansion increasingly affected Sotho-Tswana societies. Competition and conflict for resources eventually forced some chiefdoms to 'implode' into huge defensive settlements such as Molokwane,

Kaditshwene and Dithakong, which in the early 1800s housed 10 000 people or more.

Early travelers to South Africa reported that the South Sotho people were highly skilled in carving ivory and wood and they said their leatherwork was 'as soft as chamois leather'. Fragments of Sung celadon ware from the twelfth century, found at Mapungubwe, indicate a connection with China through the Limpopo waterways long before Europeans set foot in south east Africa. The traditional conical South Sotho hat also indicates oriental influence.

Chiefdoms split repeatedly, usually as a result of rivalries between contenders for the position of chief. Irregular infiltration of fugitive groups occurred from the Highveld to the Lowveld, and from Swaziland and northern KwaZulu Natal into the interior. The Lobedu, the southward moving gold-mining Venda, and small groups of Tsonga from Mozambique settled among the Sotho and a long process of cultural interaction took place

The Southern Sotho people were unified as the Basuto during the reign of King Moshoeshoe in the 1830s (read on Basuto Wars page). Moshoeshoe established control over several small groups of Sotho and Nguni speakers, who had been displaced by the *difiqane*(Zulu: *mfecane*). Some of these communities had established ties to San peoples who lived just west of Moshoeshoe's territory. As a result, the South Sotho language or *seSotho*, unlike that of North Sotho, incorporates a number of 'click' sounds associated with Khoisan languages.

By the early twentieth century, Sotho villages were losing their claims to land, largely because of pressure from Whites. Cattle raising became more difficult, and as Western economic pressures intensified, Sotho people living in Lesotho and in South Africa increasingly turned to the mines for work. By the early 1990s, an estimated 100,000 Basuto worked in South Africa's mines, and many others were part of South Africa's urban work force throughout the country.

The homelands in and around the Orange Free State

The dawn of apartheid in the 1940s marked more changes for all Black South Africans. In 1953 the South African Government introduced homelands. Southern Sotho people not living in Lesotho were assigned to the tiny homeland of QwaQwa, which borders Lesotho. QwaQwa was declared 'self-governing' in 1974, but Chief Minister Kenneth Mopeli rejected independence on the grounds that the homeland did not have a viable economy. Only about 200,000 Sotho people lived in QwaQwa during the 1980s.

A community of more than 300,000 people, Botshabelo, was incorporated into QwaQwa in 1987. Officials in the homeland capital, Phuthaditjhaba, and many homeland residents objected to the move, and the South African Supreme Court returned Botshabelo to the jurisdiction of the Orange Free State a short time later. The homeland continued to be an overcrowded enclave of people with an inadequate economic base until the homelands were dissolved in 1994.

Language, culture and beliefs

South Sotho culture, social organizations, ceremonies, language and religious beliefs are almost identical to the other two Sotho groups (Pedi and Tswana); however, there are major cultural differences between the Sotho and the Nguni (Zulu, Xhosa, Ndebele, Swazi). The Sotho people tend to group their homesteads in villages and have a technology and society that differs from the Nguni peoples.

Probably the greatest difference between Sotho and Nguni society is in contrasting marriage customs. A Sotho-speaking man often seeks a bride from a group to whom he is already related or knows well, while marriage to kin in the Nguni society is frowned upon. The Nguni are grouped in clans, while totems, or praise-names taken from animals, distinguish the Sotho-speakers.

In the past, the livelihood of the Sotho was mainly based on hunting, cultivating crops and iron smelting. Traditionally, the Sotho gave allegiance to a paramount chief and they were controlled by a hereditary district chief assisted by community headmen.

Administration of justice is still, in some respects, in the hands of these leaders. In former times, the legal code was based mainly on custom. Sotho descent rules were important, even though descent groups did not form discrete local groups. Clans were often totemic, or bound to specific natural objects or animal species by mystical relationships, sometimes involving taboos and prohibitions. Major Sotho clans included the Lion (Taung), Fish (Tlhaping), Elephant (Tloung), and Crocodile (Kwean) clans.

Community headmen's residences were clustered around the chief's residence. Sotho villages sometimes grew into large towns of several thousand people. Farmland was usually outside the village, not adjacent to the homestead. This village organization may have enabled the Sotho villagers to defend themselves more effectively than they could have with dispersed households, and it probably facilitated control over community headmen and subjects by the chief and his family.

Sotho villages were also organized into age-sets, or groups of men or women who were close in age. Each age-set had specific responsibilities e.g. men organized for warfare and herding. An entire age-set generally graduated from one task to the next, and the village often celebrated this change with a series of rituals and, in some cases, an initiation ceremony. In the past initiations into adulthood were elaborate ceremonies lasting a few months, in which girls and boys were taken separately to the bush in the winter. The boys were circumcised. Increasingly, funerals have become the most elaborate life-cycle rituals.

The Supreme Being that the Sotho people believe in is most commonly referred to as Modimo. Modimo is approached through the spirits of one's ancestors, the balimo, who are honored at ritual feasts. The ancestral spirits can bring sickness and misfortune to those who forget them or treat them disrespectfully. Today, Christianity in one form or another is accepted by most of the Sotho-speaking people. Most people in Lesotho are Catholics, but there are also many Protestant denominations. Today, many independent churches combine theses elements of African traditional religion with the doctrines of Christianity.

In Sotho tradition, the man is considered the head of the household. Women are defined as farmers and bearers of children. Polygymous marriages (more than one wife) are not uncommon among the elite, but they are rare among commoners. Marriages are arranged by transfer of bohadi (bride wealth) from the family of the groom to the family of the bride. In Sotho, the words for father (ntate) and mother (mme) are used commonly as address forms of respect for one's elders. The general attitude toward childhood is well summarized by the proverb Lefura la ngwana ke ho rungwa, which roughly translates as "Children benefit from serving their elders."

The South Sotho people of Lesotho (baSuto) are identified with the brightly colored blankets that they often wear instead of coats. These blankets have designs picturing everything from airplanes to crowns to geometric patterns. The blankets are store-bought""there is no tradition of making them locally. Traditions of folk art include beadwork, sewing, pottery making, house decoration, and weaving. Functional items such as sleeping mats, baskets, and beer strainers continue to be woven by hand from grass materials. Folk craft traditions have been revived and modified in response to the tourist trade.

The Sotho language, *seSotho*, is a Bantu language closely related to *seTswana*. Sotho utilizes click consonants in some words, while *sePedi* and *seTswana* do not have clicks. Sotho is spoken in the Kingdom of Lesotho and in South Africa. It is concentrated in the Free State, Gauteng and Eastern Cape Provinces, with small groups of speakers in Namibia and Zambia.

Sotho is 1 of the 11 official languages recognized by the South African Constitution and 7.9% of the South African population uses it as their home language. It is a tonal language governed by the noun, which is split into various classes. It is known as an agglutinating language (a combination of simple word elements to express a specific meaning), with many suffixes and prefixes used in sentence construction causing sound changes.

It is rich in proverbs, idioms, and special forms of address reserved for elders and in-laws. Currently, Sotho has two spelling systems, one in use in Lesotho and another in South Africa. For example, in Lesotho a common greeting is Khotso, le phela joang? (literally, "Peace, how are you?"). In South Africa, the word joang (how) is written jwang, and khotso is written kgotso.

Sotho was one of the first African languages to become a written language and therefore Sotho literature is extensive. South Sotho is comprised of the Fokeng, Tlokwa, Kwena, Phetla, Phuti, and Pulana dialects or varieties and according to scholars the written form was originally based on the Tlokwa dialect. Today the written language is mostly based on the Kwena and Fokeng dialects, although there are variations. Sesotho was transmuted into writing by the missionaries Casalis and Arbousset of the Paris Evangelical Mission who arrived at Thaba Bosiu in 1833. One of the first novels in a South African language was Chaka, written in Sotho by Thomas Mofolo in the early years of the twentieth century. It is still read today and has been translated into a number of languages.

Basotho Wars 1858 - 1868

The three Basotho Wars (1858-68) and the formation of Lesotho
The conflict between the Basotho people and White settlers in what is now the Free State/ Lesotho area, consisted of three wars (1858- 68). The purpose of these three wars was the maintenance of territorial rights in the area between the Caledon and Orange Rivers; from present day Wepener to Zastron, and the area north of the Caledon River, which includes present day Harrismith and the area further westwards.

The Basotho wars were preceded by the mass migration of several Nguni groups. This migration occurred during the reign of the Zulu King Shaka, who conquered several Nguni groups, which were absorbed into the Zulu kingdom. Other Nguni tribes fled and settled in other areas during this time- which is known as the Mfecane period.

In 1818, King Moshoeshoe, who was the son of the chief of the Bakotela branch of the Koena/Kwena (Crocodile) clan, helped to gain power over smaller fugitive and displaced clans. In 1820, Moshoeshoe became chief of a larger unit of Southern Sotho groups, who had fallen under his centralized authority due to competition for resources, which was intensified by a drought.

This competition for resources caused these larger groups to seek protection from other marauding groups, and Moshoeshoe and his people retreated to the mountain fortress of Thaba Bosiu in 1824. Moshoeshoe gave assistance to his defeated enemies by giving them land, which led to the establishment of the Basotho nation.

In the late 1820s, a group of Kora (a group of Khoikhoi settlers also known as the Korana) and Dutch speaking people of mixed descent arrived in the vicinity of Moshoeshoe's kingdom. As they were mounted on horseback and armed with guns, the Basotho retreated.

This also led to Moshoeshoe deciding to arm his people and give them horses.

The arrival of White settlers in the area, due to the Great Trek, was initially useful to Moshoeshoe, as the settlers created a buffer between the Basotho and the Kora. These White settlers (known as Boers) crossed the Orange River from the Cape Colony in the mid-1820s. Although these settlers allegedly asked for this permission to settle there, they later claimed it - despite Moshoeshoe's view that he had lent it to them.

In 1845 a treaty was signed, which recognised White settlement in the area; however no boundaries were drawn between the area of White settlement and Moshoeshoe's kingdom. This dispute led to inevitable border clashes and a discernible boundary became necessary.

The British, who then controlled the area between the Orange and Vaal Rivers (the Orange River Sovereignty) eventually proclaimed the Warden line (after Major Warden). This line divided territory between British territory and the Basotho under Moshoeshoe, and stretched from Cornetspruit and the Orange River through Vechtkop to Jammerbergdrift on the Caledon.

The Warden line caused much resentment, as the fertile Caledon River Valley served as a vital area in terms of agriculture for both the British and the Basotho. This border line was therefore not acceptable to Moshoeshoe, and hostility followed, which led to conflict between the Basotho and the British, who were defeated by Moshoeshoe at the battle of Viervoet in 1851. In 1851, Moshoeshoe also offered Andries Pretorius an alliance against the British in the sovereignty.

As punishment to the Basotho, Sir George Cathcart then brought troops to the Mohokane River, and Moshoeshoe was ordered to pay a fine. When he did not pay the fine in full, a battle broke out on the Berea Plateau in 1852, where the British suffered heavy losses due to the armed Basotho cavalry. This sealed the fate of the sovereignty, even though Cathcart was initially in favour of withdrawal.

In 1854, the cost of maintaining the sovereignty became too much for the British and they therefore handed over the territory to the Boers through the signing of the Sand River Convention. The Boers therefore claimed the land beyond the Caledon River, naming it the Republic of the Orange Free State. This began further conflict over land and undefined boundaries with the Basotho, who regarded themselves as the rightful owners, and who continued to use the land for grazing.

The First Basotho War

Further conflict occurred after JN Boshof; President of the OFS, and Moshoeshoe discussed issues of armed conflict and cattle rustling. However, these discussions only led to Boshof declaring war on the Basotho on 19 March 1858 (also stated as 22 March 1858). The Basotho were formidable opponents, and the Boers suffered substantial losses, as they were unable to penetrate the Basotho mountain stronghold of Thaba Bosiu (also called Thaba Bosigo). This war is also known as the First Basotho War or the War of Senekal (sometimes spelt Senegal).

During this war, the Boers also destroyed many mission stations in the Basotho kingdom, as they blamed them for educating and instilling a sense of pride among the Basotho. These mission stations had been set up by missionaries from the Paris Evangelical Society, who arrived at Thaba Bosiu in 1833. They had helped to unite the Basotho under Moshoeshoe, and were the first to write the Sesotho language.

The Second Basotho War (Seqiti War)

After this war an uneasy peace followed. J.H Brand, who replaced Boshoff, took initiative and negotiated with Moshoeshoe, who objected that the frontier was not clear. However, hostilities re-surfaced, and President Brand believed that the OFS should use its military superiority against the Basotho.

Moshoeshoe had also realized his precarious position, and had applied for British protection from Sir Philip Wodehouse, a new commissioner who had arrived in the Cape in 1861.

The Warden Line had then been reaffirmed, and although the Basotho were given time to withdraw, attacks continued later nonetheless. In 1865, the Orange Free State launched the Second Basotho War known in Sesotho as the Seqiti War. The word seqiti refers to the sound made by the new cannon the Boers used to crush the Basotho strongholds, mainly in the present day Free State province.

The Free State army then began to seize cattle and destroy crops, and two attempts were then made to storm Moshoeshoe's stronghold at Thaba Bosiu, where Commandant Wepener was killed.

Moshoeshoe was then compelled to accept the peace of Thaba Bosiu on 11 April 1866, due an exhaustion of Basotho food supplies. Moshoeshoe's son Molapo had also allegedly concluded a separate peace treaty.

Moshoeshoe then renewed entreaties for British protection after a short armistice. This was because due to the fact that the Free State Government was late in allocating land, the Basotho slowly advanced over the border line, and further tensions mounted. The Free State

Government began to raise an armed force, which was aggravated by the murder of two Whites in Ladybrand in June 1867.

The Third Basotho War

Brand demanded the hand over of the murderers, but Moshoeshoe stated that he had not agreed to the frontier line of 1866, and therefore the events had not occurred on Free State territory. In July 1867, the third war between the Free State and the Basotho in ten years began, and Boer forces overran Moshoeshoe's land and conquered all the land except the impregnable fortress of Thaba Bosiu.

The Free State forces had achieved great military success, and Moshoeshoe was compelled to ask for British assistance. Basutoland was then annexed on 12 March 1868, after Governor Wodehouse received instructions to negotiate with Moshoeshoe for the recognition of the Basotho as British subjects.

On the 12 March 1868, the British parliament declared the Basotho Kingdom a British protectorate. The Orange Free State was forced to discontinue the war if it was not to raise trouble with the British Empire.

In February 1869, the boundaries of present day Lesotho (previously Basutoland) were then drawn up according to the Convention of Aliwal-North. This convention gave the Conquered Territory to the Free State, and the boundary line was moved further south to Langeberg. No further armed conflict between the Free State and the Basotho took place after this.

As a result, King Moshoeshoe was able to save his kingdom from being overrun by the Boers. King Moshoeshoe died two years in 1870, after the end of war, and was buried at the summit of Thaba Bosiu.

Griqua

The arrival of the Boers and the colonial masters to the area known as Griqualand West, denied the Griquas the opportunity of following their own development paths. They lost their land and traditional resources, and were tossed into a sea of rapid social change which saw them lose the independence they had searched for in the Orange Free State area.

In the course of the 18th century, new communities defined by race, culture, religion and differential access to land and power began to emerge; they became tied together through the spoken word. One of these communities was the "Bastaards" which referred to offspring of liaisons between Europeans, slaves and Khoikhoi. The term was also used to refer to subordinate Blacks who could speak Dutch, ride and shoot.

On White owned farms, Bastaards or Basters, did more skilled jobs such as transport riders and craftsmen. They took these skills with them later into the interior. The term "Bastaards" originally denoted people with a greater "civilisation" and attachment to Christianity than the Khoikhoi or slaves.

In the second half of the 18th century, small Baster communities formed in the fringe areas of the northwest and the eastern frontier – Colesberg, Hantam, Roggeveld and Namaqualand. They could speak Afrikaans, had European names and their children were baptised in the church. They were even called up to do commando service. Notwithstanding these facts, they were increasingly being squeezed out from the land they held and they rarely succeeded in winning land claims as burghers invariably had the stronger claim, and better access to the field cornets who reported on any such claims. Basters and other people of mixed race moved first to the outer limits of the colony and then beyond its borders.

Origins:

The Griquas could trace their forefathers to two clans, the Koks and Barendse, the first made up mainly of Khoikhoi and the second of mixed European descent.

A freed slave, Adam Kok, who managed to obtain burgher rights and a farm near the present Piketberg, founded the most vigorous mixed community. According to one tradition, Adam Kok married the daughter of the chief of a Khoikhoi clan, the Chariguriqua, during the 1750's. He attracted a following as he moved up from Piketberg to Little Namaqualand and by the 1790's Cornelius Kok, Adams' son moved out of the colony to the Orange River and then eastwards along the bank to what is now known as Griqualand West. Cornelius had gathered with him a large number of Basters, some Khoikhoi and escaped slaves.

The two groups, under their respective leaders Cornelius and the brothers Barend and Nicolaas Barends roamed the area around the Orange River until 1804 when they were persuaded by two missionaries from the London Missionary Society to settle down with their followers north of the Orange River.

Adam Kok, leader of the Griquas at Nomansland

On the insistence of the missionary John Campbell, they came up with the name Griqua. They established a basic system of government based on leaders known as *kaptyns* and magistrates drawn from the leading families. Prominent families included were the Kok and Barends families, and the Waterboer family complex.

These families maintained stability by taking on a life of raiding and establishing trade links with their neighbours. It was alleged that Andries Waterboer had no White parentage but was a dependent of Adam Kok. Later, he allied himself to the church, acting as an interpreter and rose to influence after 1820 when he was appointed *kaptyn*. The Griquas attempted to achieve a greater measure of political autonomy by inviting the missionaries to join them.

The Griquas founded a settlement called Klaarwater, later known as Griquatown. The Griqua communities were constantly bedevilled with internal divisions and environmental uncertainty. One of the greatest causes of tension was between wanting to be within the colonial fold with its security and economic opportunities versus wanting to maintain independence. The missionaries wanted to Christianise the Griqua which would basically transform them into a settled agricultural and pastoral group. By drawing up a constitution, the *kaptyns* lost much of their power. Even though this created tension, it accorded the Griqua a degree of respectability while the missionaries offered some protection.

Poor relations between Waterboer and the Kok and Barends family complex caused Adam Kok II and Barend Barends to move away from Griquatown with their followers to Cambell and Danielskuil, respectively. Later Barends moved to Boetsap and the Koks to Philippolis. This made Andries Waterboer the dominant Griqua in Griquatown itself and the protégé of the missionaries.

The Griquas were the first people from the Cape to settle in the Transorangia area, beyond the Orange River. Some Griqua raided the Tlhaping, a Tswana speaking community, while others obtained cattle from them which was used to trade with the Cape farmers for firearms, horses and wagons,. The Griqua also acted as middlemen in a lucrative ivory trade between the Tswana and the colony, while others hunted ivory for themselves.

The Boers and Griqualand West

The Boers arrived in the area of Griquatown after Natal was taken over by the British. They acquired land from the Griqua, buying it in exchange for horses, liquor, firearms and ammunition. Trouble started when Kok arrested a Boer accused of ill-treating his people, and the trekker community tried to take over his entire territory. A British force stationed at Colesberg, quickly crossed the Orange River and defeated the settlers at Zwartkoppies.

Maitland, who was Governor at the time, decided to put an end to the territorial ambitions of the Boers by inventing a complicated system of land tenure whereby each chief's land would be divided into two parts: one to be occupied by the chief and his people, and the other by the Boers who would pay rent to the chief and the Cape government.

Kok quickly agreed to this plan as it ensured that all regions south of the Riet River would remain inalienable Griqua property, while the area north of the river, although remaining under his control, would be leased by the Boers who were British subjects. In 1845, Maitland appointed a British Resident to Transorangia to oversee the implementation of this system, a job which Major Douglas Warden took over.

Maitland's time as Governor came to an end in 1847 and was replaced by Sir Henry Pottinger, who was then soon replaced by Sir Henry George Wakelyn Smith. Smith rebuked Maitland's system of land tenure and declared that all rent from White tenant farmers on Griqua land north of the Riet River would divert to the Crown. In addition, Whites would be allowed to obtain farms to the south of the river in an area, in terms of Maitland's system, that could never be settled by Whites. Smith suitably humbled Adam Kok into acceptance of these terms.

By 1861, the Griquas, tired of the constant friction with their Dutch neighbours in the Orange Free State, sold them their lands, before settling in the territory of Griqualand East. In 1867, the discovery of diamonds near Hopetown brought about enormous changes in the social and economic make-up of the region. Overnight the area became flooded with fortune-seekers from Europe, North America and Australia. The ownership of this area became the subject of conflicting claims from the Khoikhoi, Tswana and Dutch groups.

In March 1871, the diamond field claims were resolved in favour of the Khoikhoi leader Nicolaas Waterboer, who immediately petitioned the British for the annexation of his lands to the Cape Colony. As a result, on 27 October 1871 the diamond fields were proclaimed a British territory under the name of Griqualand West.

The Griquas derived no benefit from this; they were merely pawns in the hands of the Imperial authorities who were trying to acquire control over the mineral rich lands. In November 1876, Lieutenant-Governor Lanyon cleverly embarked on a surveying process with the intention of confining indigenous Black people to strategically placed rural locations which comprised about ten percent of the original Griqualand. The divisions of Barkley West, Hay, Herbert and Kimberley were probably proclaimed at about the same time.

However, the Cape Government, faced with the objections of both European settlers and indigenous residents, refused to incorporate the territory, and in 1873 Griqualand West was proclaimed a separate Crown Colony with its capital at Kimberley.

In 1876, Chief Waterboer, in whose name the diamond fields had been annexed, was arrested and imprisoned when he tried to free some of his followers from a prison work gang. On 5 August 1879, the Cape Parliament passed a Bill of Annexation, which was only implemented on 18 October 1880 (SESA 1972). A census taken in Griqualand West in 1877 revealed that the province had a total of 44,877 residents, of whom 12,374 were of European descent.

Griqualand East

In 1860, Adam Kok III trekked from the vicinity of Philippolis, where they had lost their lands to the emigrant Boers, to find a new home. They arrived in 1862 in the territory known as No Man's Land, between the Cape and Natal. They lived in a larger for some ten years before founding their town of Kokstad.

Insecure and distrustful, in 1869 Adam Kok requested that the territory of Griqualand East be annexed by the British, with the specific stipulation that it should not be brought under the direct rule of Natal even though he was granted full title to the land and total autonomy of government. Accordingly Griqualand was taken over in 1874, and although the Act of Annexation was passed by the Cape Parliament in 1877, it was not promulgated until 17 September 1879. The territory was initially divided into four magisterial districts centred at Matatiele, Mount Frere, Umzimkulu and Kokstad, later renamed Mount Currie.

Throughout the 1870s, Griqualand East, and its surrounding territories, were the object of competing tribal interests and complex political alliances. As a result, the British found it difficult to implement effective colonial rule over the region until the remainder of Pondoland was also brought under their control. The lands of the Xesibe, centred at Mount Ayliff, were brought under their administration in 1878, but were not annexed to the Cape Colony until 25 October 1886.

In 1886, a small pocket of land called the Rode Valley was purchased from the Mpondo chief Umquikela, and was added to Mount Ayliff by Act No 45 of 1887, which was confirmed on 15 September 1888. The annexation of Pondoland to the Cape was completed under Act No 5 of 1894, provisions of which also ceded a portion of western Pondoland to Griqualand East. As a result of this transfer the divisions of Mount Fletcher, Qumbu, Tsolo and Maclear were brought under its administration.

The Griquas soon became a minority in the area and soon began to sell their properties to both European settlers and Pondo farmers, who were beginning to prosper there. The census of 1891 indicated that Griqualand East had a population of 152 618 persons, of whom 9 071 were literate. By 1904, these figures had risen to 222 685 and 21 146 respectively.

By 1917, the surviving Griqua people, highly demoralized by their loss of independence, once more trekked to a site near Touws River in the Karoo but their attempt to find a new community failed and most returned to Kokstad

The Khoikhoi

In around 2300 BP (Before Present), hunter-gatherers called the San acquired domestic stock in what is now modern day Botswana. Their population grew, and spread throughout the Western half of South Africa. They were the first pastoralists in southern Africa, and called themselves Khoikhoi (or Khoe), which means 'men of men' or 'the real people'. This name was chosen to show pride in their past and culture. The Khoikhoi brought a new way of life to South Africa and to the San, who were hunter-gatherers as opposed to herders. This led to misunderstandings and subsequent conflict between the two groups.

The Khoikhoi were the first native people to come into contact with the Dutch settlers in the mid 17th century. As the Dutch took over land for farms, the Khoikhoi were dispossessed, exterminated, or enslaved and therefore their numbers dwindled. The Khoikhoi were called the 'Hottentots' by European settlers because the sound of their language was so different from any European language, and they could not pronounce many of the words and sounds.

The Khoikhoi used a word while dancing that sounded like 'Hottentots' and therefore settlers referred to the Khoikhoi by this name – however today this term is considered derogatory. The settlers used the term 'Bushmen' for the San, a term also considered derogatory today. Many of those whom the colonists called 'Bushmen' were in fact Khoikhoi or former Khoikhoi. For this reason, scholars sometimes find it convenient to refer to hunters and herders together as 'Khoisan'.

When European settlement began, Khoikhoi groups called the Namaqua were settled in modern day Namibia and the north-eastern Cape; others, including the Korana, along the Orange River; and the Gonaqua, interspersed among the Xhosa in the Eastern Cape. But the largest concentration of Khoikhoi, numbering in the tens of thousands inhabited the well-watered pasture lands of the south-western Cape. These 'Cape' Khoikhoi would be the first African population to bear the brunt of White settlement.

Nomadic heritage:

The Khoikhoi kept herds of animals such as goat, cattle and sheep and had to move around to find enough grazing land for their animals. They moved according to the seasons and only stayed in one place for a few weeks. This meant that they had to be able to carry all their belongings themselves, or load them onto the backs of their animals.

Houses had to be very light and easy to erect and take apart. For this reason they were made of thin poles covered with reed mats. Even pots and buckets were made of wood with small handles to make them easier to tie to animals' backs. They also wore clothes made of leather, like the San.

The animals, especially cattle, were a sign of wealth and the Khoikhoi only ate cattle that had died or had been stolen from their enemies. They only killed their own animals for important occasions like funerals or weddings. The women milked the animals and gathered wild plants from the veld and the men killed game for everyday food. This shows that the Khoikhoi hunted and gathered, but also herded animals.

Khoikhoi society and language:

Khoikhoi society consisted of both rich and poor, as animals – which were a sign of wealth - could belong to individuals. This is because animals provided food, clothes and transport. This was completely different from the San, who were all considered equal and shared everything. Wealthier Khoikhoi people would share their milk with poorer members of their group, but would still be considered more important. They would also rub animal fat over their bodies to show their wealth.

Khoisan languages, characterised by implosive consonants or 'clicks', belonged to a totally different language family from those of the Bantu speakers. In contrast to the San who spoke highly divergent languages, the Khoikhoi spoke closely related dialects of the same language. NÁ má, previously called Hottentot, is the most populous and widespread of the Khoikhoi and San languages. It belongs to the Khoe language family, and is spoken in Namibia, Botswana, and South Africa by the Namaqua, Damara, and Hai'om, as well as smaller ethnic groups such as the Khomani (to read more about the language see the history of the San).

The Kora:

The Korana or Kora were a nomadic Khoikhoi group that probably derived their name from a chief called Kora (or Gora), who was originally a leader of the Gorachouqua (`-qua' meaning 'people of'). This leader detached himself from this group with his followers and became the first great chief of the Korana. Others say that the name Korana could mean 'the real thing'.

Initially there were two main groups, the Great Korana and the Little Korana. Each of these broke into splinter groups that divided until there were many groups whose names have been slowly forgotten or were not recorded. Quarrels over water and grazing rights, or the ownership of women or livestock usually caused the divisions amongst groups. When parties split up they usually assumed the name of their leader. But sometimes they took the name of a place where they had stayed for a long time.

One such case was the name Hoogekraal (`High Kraal'), the original name for Pacaltsdorp, near George. Korana family names tended to signify a special characteristic or occupation such as the Towenaars (Sorcerers) and the Regshande (Right-handers). Where the first Chief Kora lived is unknown, but in early times, most Korana lived near the Gariep, Vaal and Harts rivers and others moved into the Overberg and the Karoo.

The last great Korana trek took place during the late 17th century, when they trekked from their chiefdoms in the south-western Cape to escape pressure from White settlers. These Korana trekkers travelled along the western trading routes as far north as the great river that they called Gariep, which means 'river'. The early pioneers added 'Groot' (Great) to it, and after that, it was simply known as the Groot Rivier. A Dutch soldier of Scottish extraction, Robert Jacob Gordon, who was commander of the garrison at the Cape in 1777, renamed it the Orange after the Prince of Orange. However, many still referred to it as the Groot Rivier. After the 1994 change of government, it was given back its original name, Gariep.

For many centuries the early people lived along this river and its tributaries because game was able to graze in the vleie and the berry trees and bulbous plants grew in profusion. There, the Korana settled among the Nama herders and groups of San hunter-gatherers. By then, the Korana had become well-armed and some sources cite that they lived very much in the style of the 'Wild West'. They knew how to ride horses, understood the value of keeping their mounts in prime condition, and frequently raided the farms south of the great river and the Baster communities.

They also settled in what is today the Free State, the district that became known as Koranaland (Gordonia). Many small conflicts over hunting and plundering took place between these groups and the Bantu-speaking peoples and White trekkers in the area. It is important to note however, that livestock raids were carried out by a minority group of Korana.

An important leader at the time was Karel Ruyter or Ruiters, an escaped slave, who became chief of the Hoengei group of Gona in the Zuurveld in the mid-eighteenth century. Other leaders were Piet Rooi, Jan Kupido, Klaas Lukas and Pofadder. Klaas Lukas, who had his headquarters at Olyvenhoutsdrift (Upington), was the most powerful chief.

The small conflicts over cattle and land raids came to a head in 1868, when the colonial government created a special magisterial district. The Northern Border Protection Act was passed to permit action against the Korana. A special border unit was stationed at Kenhardt, but the handful of police and burghers were too few to protect a 330 km stretch of land. This eventually led to the Korana wars of 1869 and 1878.

In 1869, the Frontier Armed and Mounted Police and a small detachment of the Royal Artillery arrived in the area - led by Sir Walter Currie. Together with 400 mounted Boers and Basters, 100 Xhosa and 200 regulars, Currie was soon able to scatter the Korana – but the eluded capture. Klaas Lukas eventually captured the Korana 'raid' leaders and handed them over to the colonial authorities, who banished them to Robben Island. Later, a prolonged drought forced White settlers and Coloured farmers, as well as the Korana, to move closer to the Gariep River. Such a conglomeration of herds close made it easy for Korana 'raider' groups to prey on the herds, and their activities aroused the ire of the district.

Klaas Lukas, who was initially neutral, gathered together 1,000-armed men to defend their livestock. His supporters included the majority of the Korana, the Nama Afrikanders led by Jacobus Afrikander, and a number of Griqua rebels under Gamka Pienaar. The Korana 'raider' groups were defeated and came under the control of the Cape Government. Those Korana who rejected a future under colonial rule trekked further into the Kalahari. The Cape Government settled the Basters near Upington to form a buffer between the Boers and the Korana. Today, the Korana have almost completely disappeared as a separate group through assimilation with the population in the area.

'Bastaards' or 'Baster' was a derogatory referred to offspring of liaisons between Europeans, slaves and Khoikhoi. The term was also used to refer to subordinate Blacks who could speak Dutch, ride and shoot.

Indian South Africans

From bondage to freedom: The 150th anniversary of the arrival of Indian workers in South Africa

The feature on Indian South Africans forms part of our larger feature on the People of South Africa. It is a long term project to build a comprehensive overview of the rich diversity of peoples, traditions and culture that address the question, 'Who are South Africans?' This year, 2010, is the 150th anniversary of the arrival of the Indian indentured labourers and the birth of this community in South Africa. We are using this to launch and major project to build a comprehensive social and political history of this African community.

Origins:

South Africans of Indian origin comprise a heterogeneous community distinguished by different origins, languages, and religious beliefs. The first Indians arrived during the Dutch colonial era, as slaves, in 1684. A conservative calculation based strictly on records shows over 16 300 slaves from the Indian subcontinent having been brought to the Cape. In the decades 1690 to 1725 over 80% of the slaves were Indians. This practice continued until the end of slavery in 1838. They made up the majority of slaves that came from the Far East and were by the 1880s totally integrated into the Cape White and Coloured communities.

In the second half if the 19th Century, Indians came to South Africa in two categories, namely as indentured workers in 1860 and later as 'free' or 'passenger' Indians. The former came as a result of a triangular pact among three governments, which stated that the indentured Indians were to work for the Natal colonial government on Natal's sugar plantations. The 'free' Indians came to South Africa mainly as traders alert to new opportunities abroad. These 'free Indians' came at their own expense from India, Mauritius, and other places. However, emigration was stopped in 1914.

Between November 1860 and 1911(when the system of indentured labour was stopped) nearly 152 184 indentured labourers from across India arrived in Natal. After serving their indentures, the first category of Indians were free to remain in South Africa or to return to India. By 1910, nearly 26.85% indentured men returned to India, but most chose to stay and thus constituted the forbearers of the majority of present-day South African Indians.

With 1994 and the advent of a democratic constitution, immigration policy restrictions, imposed by the apartheid regime, were scrapped. People from India, Pakistan, Sri Lanka and Bangladesh, arrived in South Africa as new immigrants. However, there is a major cultural division between these new groups and Indian South Africans.

A key factor that helped forge a common South African "Indian" identity was the political struggles waged against harsh discriminatory laws enacted against Indians and the other Black oppressed groups in the country. As a consequence, the Indian community established a number of political formations, the most prominent being the Natal Indian Congress (NIC) established by Gandhi in 1894, and the Transvaal and Cape Indian Congresses in the early part of the 20th century. Members of the Indian Congress, together with socialist activists in the Communist Party of South Africa were instrumental, from the 1930s, in building cross racial alliances. The small Indian, Coloured and White progressive sectors joined with progressive

African activists and together, they conducted a common non-racial struggle for Freedom and Equality.

Language, culture and beliefs:

English is spoken as a first language by most Indian South Africans, although a minority of the Indian South African population, especially the elders, still speak some Indian languages. These languages include Hindi, Tamil, Telugu, Urdu, Punjabi, and Gujarati. Indian South Africans are predominantly Hindu, but Muslims, Christians, and Sikhs also came to South Africa from India from as early as 1860.

Hindu, the most prominent religion in India, originated 5000 years ago. The Hindu religion prescribes a three fold approach to serving God. This approach includes knowledge, or the studying of the Bhagavad-Gita and other texts; yoga, to connect both body and mind, and devotion or *bhakti*, which promotes serving God through prayer and benevolent acts. Notable Hindu festivals include Diwali/Deepavali, the festival of lights, and the Tamil Thai Poosam Kavady annual festival.

Muslim/Islamic influence began in South Africa with the arrival of indentured workers from the west and south coast of India. As only 7-10% of these workers were Muslim, Sheikh Ahmad, the founding father of Islam in Natal, and later Soofie Saheb ensured that impoverished Muslim Indians were not drawn to Hinduism. Therefore, a concerted effort was made to retain their religious heritage, through the demarcation of Islamic festivals and the establishment of Muslim schools or *madrasahs*.

The Islamic community continues to thrive in South Africa, in both Natal and the Western Cape - where indentured labourers moved with their families after the completion of their contracts. Followers of the Muslim faith are committed to praying at least five times a day, and are not permitted to drink alcohol. Notable Muslim celebrations include Eid, and Ramadan.

The Sikh faith forms a slender portion of the local population, and is a religion influenced by both Hindu and Islam. The Sikh religion is concerned with a belief in *One Immortal Being* and ten gurus. Many Sikhs wear an iron or steel bracelet as a symbol of their devotion to their religion. Originating in the Punjab region, prominent Sikh celebrations include Parkash Utsav, which celebrates *'Divine Light'* or *'Divine Knowledge'*.

The diverse Indian population in South Africa is concentrated in Kwa-Zulu Natal's largest city, Durban, which has the most substantial Indian population in sub-Saharan Africa. South Africa as a whole also has a substantial Indian population, with over 1 million people of Indian descent. Therefore, Indian influences have contributed to the multi-cultural diversity of South Africa. The local culinary landscape has been infused with a diverse array of Oriental flavour - most notably in the Natal region. Popular dishes include curry, and an intrinsic Durban dish called 'bunny chow', which is half a loaf of bread, hollowed out and filled with curry.

South African Indians retain a sense of cultural and social connection to India, and a concept of primary local and secondary ancestral identity is prevalent among people of Indian descent.

Kora

The Korana or Kora were a nomadic Khoikhoi group that probably derived their name from a chief called Kora (or Gora), who was originally a leader of the Gorachouqua (`-qua' meaning 'people of'). This leader detached himself from this group with his followers and became the first great chief of the Korana. Others say that the name Korana could mean 'the real thing'.

Initially there were two main groups, the Great Korana and the Little Korana. Each of these broke into splinter groups that divided until there were many groups whose names have been slowly forgotten or were not recorded. Quarrels over water and grazing rights, or the ownership of women or livestock usually caused the divisions amongst groups. When parties split up they usually assumed the name of their leader. But sometimes they took the name of a place where they had stayed for a long time.

One such case was the name Hoogekraal (`High Kraal'), the original name for Pacaltsdorp, near George. Korana family names tended to signify a special characteristic or occupation such as the Towenaars (Sorcerers) and the Regshande (Right-handers). Where the first Chief Kora lived is unknown, but in early times, most Korana lived near the Gariep, Vaal and Harts rivers and others moved into the Overberg and the Karoo.

The last great Korana trek took place during the late 17th century, when they trekked from their chiefdoms in the south-western Cape to escape pressure from White settlers. These Korana trekkers travelled along the western trading routes as far north as the great river that they called Gariep, which means 'river'. The early pioneers added 'Groot' (Great) to it, and after that, it was simply known as the Groot Rivier. A Dutch soldier of Scottish extraction, Robert Jacob Gordon, who was commander of the garrison at the Cape in 1777, renamed it the Orange after the Prince of Orange. However, many still referred to it as the Groot Rivier. After the 1994 change of government, it was given back its original name, Gariep.

For many centuries the early people lived along this river and its tributaries because game was able to graze in the vleie and the berry trees and bulbous plants grew in profusion. There, the Korana settled among the Nama herders and groups of San hunter-gatherers. By then, the Korana had become well-armed and some sources cite that they lived very much in the style of the 'Wild West'. They knew how to ride horses, understood the value of keeping their mounts in prime condition, and frequently raided the farms south of the great river and the Baster communities.

They also settled in what is today the Free State, the district that became known as Koranaland (Gordonia). Many small conflicts over hunting and plundering took place between these groups and the Bantu-speaking peoples and White trekkers in the area. It is important to note however, that livestock raids were carried out by a minority group of Korana.

An important leader at the time was Karel Ruyter or Ruiters, an escaped slave, who became chief of the Hoengei group of Gona in the Zuurveld in the mid-eighteenth century. Other leaders were Piet Rooi, Jan Kupido, Klaas Lukas and Pofadder. Klaas Lukas, who had his headquarters at Olyvenhoutsdrift (Upington), was the most powerful chief.

The small conflicts over cattle and land raids came to a head in 1868, when the colonial government created a special magisterial district. The Northern Border Protection Act was passed to permit action against the Korana. A special border unit was stationed at Kenhardt, but the handful of police and burghers were too few to protect a 330 km stretch of land. This eventually led to the Korana wars of 1869 and 1878.

In 1869, the Frontier Armed and Mounted Police and a small detachment of the Royal Artillery arrived in the area - led by Sir Walter Currie. Together with 400 mounted Boers and Basters, 100 Xhosa and 200 regulars, Currie was soon able to scatter the Korana – but the eluded capture. Klaas Lukas eventually captured the Korana 'raid' leaders and handed them over to the colonial authorities, who banished them to Robben Island. Later, a prolonged drought forced White settlers and Coloured farmers, as well as the Korana, to move closer to the Gariep River. Such a conglomeration of herds close made it easy for Korana 'raider' groups to prey on the herds, and their activities aroused the ire of the district.

Klaas Lukas, who was initially neutral, gathered together 1,000-armed men to defend their livestock. His supporters included the majority of the Korana, the Nama Afrikanders led by Jacobus Afrikander, and a number of Griqua rebels under Gamka Pienaar. The Korana 'raider' groups were defeated and came under the control of the Cape Government. Those Korana who rejected a future under colonial rule trekked further into the Kalahari. The Cape Government settled the Basters near Upington to form a buffer between the Boers and the Korana. Today, the Korana have almost completely disappeared as a separate group through assimilation with the population in the area.

'Bastaards' or 'Baster' was a derogatory referred to offspring of liaisons between Europeans, slaves and Khoikhoi. The term was also used to refer to subordinate Blacks who could speak Dutch, ride and shoot.

Ndebele

Early History

Few Southern African indigenous groups have so captured the interest of the world as have the South ama Ndebele of the central highveld, an area previously known as the Transvaal but today incorporated into the Gauteng and Northern Provinces. Their highly colourful and intricately painted homesteads, their skilled and varied beadwork, their clear language of architecture, and their stately forms of dress have made them a popular field of research with artists, architects and social anthropologists. They have also become a major focus of interest for many visitors to this country.

It is generally accepted today that the South Ndebele migrated onto the central highveld of southern Africa some four centuries ago. The exact date of their arrival is difficult to determine, but estimates tend to vary from 1485 by Fourie, through to the 1630-1670 period established by Van Warmelo. The latter dating is today regarded as the more reliable of the two.

Both Fourie and Van Warmelo are in agreement that, despite the fact that the Ndebele settled in a predominantly Sotho-Tswana speaking area, they have retained their customs and Nguni language roots with "remarkable tenacity". However some researchers have suggested a Sotho influence in some rituals and aspects of material culture, and more recent research into their architecture, settlement patterns, and methods of construction seem to indicate a definite Pedi-Tswana influence, even allowing for the adaptations one has come to expect of a culture moving from the grass-rich coastal lands east of the

Drakensberge to the more extreme thermal variations found on the South African Highveld.

Details regarding the Ndebele prior to their arrival on the highveld are scarce, and their recorded history only begins with the names of their first two kings, Mafana and Mhlanga. Following Mhlanga's death the clan became embroiled in a protracted struggle which eventually brought his son, Musi, to the leadership. By that stage the group had already moved to Mnyamana, near Wonderboompoort, immediately north of the future Boer town of Pretoria. Musi, in his turn, had five sons: Manala, Masombuka, Ndzundza, Mathombeni and Dhlomu.

Upon his death Musi was buried beneath a tree at Wonderboompoort, a location which is still visited by his descendants to the present day. Almost inevitably his sons quarreled over their inheritance and, as a result, the clan split into a number of smaller groups, the largest two coalescing under the leaderships of Manala and Ndzundza respectively. Masombuka left briefly but rejoined Manala later on, while Dhlomu and some of his followers are reputed to have returned to KwaZulu. For the purpose of subsequent Ndebele history the Manala were held to be the senior of the two groups.

In due course Ndzundza was succeeded by his son Mxetsha who, in his turn, was succeeded by his son Magoboli. Magoboli was followed by his son Bongwe, who unfortunately only reigned for three years, and as a result of his premature death, his brother Sindeni was appointed as regent. At this time, for reasons that are not known, there was a shift in the line of succession, which allowed Sindeni's son, Mahlangu, to follow his father. As a result the ruling family, which had previously been known as the Mdungwa, now became the Mahlangu. The last of these events probably took place in the latter part of the mid-eighteenth century.

Mahlangu was succeeded by his son Phaswana, who was followed in his turn by Maridili, who was followed in rapid order by his four sons, Mdalanyana, Mgwezana, Dzele and Mxabule. The last, Mxabule, was murdered by his nephew Magodongo, the son of his older brother Mgwezana, who then became head of the Ndzundza. In 1823 the amaKumalo under Mzilikazi invaded the highveld, and in about 1825 they attacked the Ndzundza, burning their capital at Mnyamana, and killing Magodongo together with all his sons from his Right-hand House. The remnants of the Ndzundza fled from Mnyamana under the leadership of Mabhogo, a younger son of Magodongo and the only survivor of his Left-hand House, and settled at Namashaxelo, near the site of the latter-day Boer village of Roossenekal. At this time Mabhogo, who ruled until 1865, entered into an alliance with the neighbouring Pedi chief Malewa, and it seems probable that the alterations in Ndebele material culture can be dated from this time onwards.

In 1847 Mabhogo was visited for the first time by groups of disaffected Dutch farmers from the Cape, better known as Voortrekkers, who rapidly came to know the Ndebele as either the Mapog, Mapogga, Mapoers, Mapoch or M'pogga. Although most Ndebele today find this form of address derogatory, many South Africans sadly still persist with this form of address.

Almost from the onset sporadic skirmishes began to take place between these new immigrants, or Boers as they became known, and the Ndebele-Pedi alliance, who actively resisted the incursions which they were beginning to make upon their ancestral lands. In 1864 the alliance was attacked, and defeated, by a Swazi force acting at the instigation of the Boers, leaving the Dutch in the rear-guard to conduct a simple mopping-up operation of survivors. Soon thereafter, in 1865, Mabhogo died, leaving the Ndebele to sort out a complex and bitter inheritance struggle. As a result Ndebele leadership passed to the Masilela family. Soqaleni ruled until 1873, followed by Xobongo, a tyrant who ruled until 1879, when he was succeeded by Nyabele.

Origins of the name "Ndebele"

The name, Ndebele, was probably derived from the Sotho-Tswana term "tebele", meaning a stranger, or one who plunders. They share in this appellation with at least three other South African groups, the most famous being the amaKumalo, an Nguni-speaking group who, under the leadership of Mzilikazi, migrated from northern KwaZulu in 1823, and after a residence of some thirteen years on the highveld, moved to western Zimbabwe in 1837, where they became know by the Shona variant of Matabele. The name has also been applied to the North Ndebele, originally a Venda-speaking group who settled in the Pietersburg area and became acculturised by their Sotho-speaking neighbours; and the baTlokwa, a Sotho-speaking group who joined the British invasion of KwaZulu in 1879, and in consequence were awarded land in the Nqutu region of KwaZulu-Natal. The term is therefore consistent with the idea of being a stranger, an invader, or perhaps even a refugee into a region.

A brief history of polygamy in Southern Africa

One of the preconceptions more popularly held by both academics and lay public alike in regard to southern African rural society is that the indigenous family unit is polygamous in nature. This is only partly true. A broad survey of homestead patterns in the region reveals that whilst a number of polygamous settlements may still be found in the rural countryside, these are in a distinct minority, and monogamous marriages appear to be the general norm. It could of course be argued that this is a recent development brought about by the work of Christian missionaries, but the validity of such an assumption needs be questioned. Not only do the Christian churches which enjoy the largest following in southern Africa, the so-called Independent Churches, permit their followers to practice polygamy, but although the practice of polygamy was indeed more prevalent during the last century, its presence was not as widespread as various missionaries way have wished us to believe. Lichtenstein wrote of the Xhosa in 1812 that:

"Most of the Koossas have but one wife; the kings and chiefs of the kraals only have four or five."

This was reinforced by Alberti who stated, also of the Xhosa, that:

"Those with least resources, must be satisfied with one woman, others have two, and rarely more."

Contemporary visitors to other parts of the country have come to similar conclusions. Livingstone went one step further and in 1857 estimated that approximately 43% of Tswana men practiced polygamy, and then only a very small minority of these had more than three wives. By 1946 an official census revealed that this figure had dropped to 11% with only 1.3% having three wives or more.

The practice of polygamy may, in most cases, be explained in terms of a levirate, a social practice, used to ensure the continued status and survival of widows and orphans within an established family structure. While it is true, therefore, that every rural family is potentially polygamous in nature, we need to question whether such polygamy was the result of "male sexuality and lust", as the missionaries would have it, or merely the enforcement of social obligations intended to reinforce ties between family or clan groupings. Recent data would seem to show that some 27% of rural households are currently headed by widowed or single women.

If we were to assume that in the 1850s an equivalent number of women could have become widows and were thus absorbed into the monogamous households of family members, thus making them polygamous, then it will be seen that this form of union could have accounted for most of the polygamous marriages recorded by Livingstone among the Tswana. The remaining group, those with three wives or more, were a distinct minority and their polygamy may be explained in terms of group leaders creating political alliances and gaining control of resources for their own communities.

The general trend away from polygamous unions evidenced since 1900 could therefore be explained in two ways. The growth of urbanisation and the establishment of urban-based political structures has brought about a decreased emphasis upon both regional group identity and the power of the traditional and inherited rural leadership. The need for making unions based upon political expediency has thus lessened considerably. The economics of obtaining a bride in the rural areas has also changed substantially over the past five generations, as women also began to enter the ranks of an industrialised and urban proletariat in increasing numbers after the 1930s.

The conclusion therefore is that the practice of polygamy may have been common in southern Africa up to the end of the last century but that it was never as widespread as has been popularly represented.

The ZAR war against the Ndzundza Ndebele

The leadership of Nyabele was to mark the final era of Ndzundza Ndebele independence. On 13 August 1882 the Pedi paramount chief Sekhukhune was killed, together with fourteen of his advisors. The assassins were acting at the behest of Mampuru, Sehukhune's half brother, who had previously contested the Pedi chieftainship in 1861, and who, under the British administration of the Transvaal, had acted as chief during Sekhukhune's imprisonment in Pretoria from 1879 to 1881.

The ZAR Government, conscious of its newly-won independence from the British, was determine to exercise its authority over the Pedi and demanded that Mampuru be handed over for trial. Mampuru then fled and sought refuge with the Ndzundza, who had previously supported him in 1861 in his claim for the Pedi leadership. The Volksraad of the ZAR demanded his apprehension, but Nyabele not only declined to hand over Mampuru, but also refused to pay the customary Hut Tax to the new Transvaal government. Although largely symbolic, this gesture was also an open act of defiance which proclaimed Ndzundza independence from the ZAR and refuted Boer claims of suzerainty over his people.

Given their precarious hold over their indigenous subjects, this was not a challenge which the newly established ZAR could afford to ignore, Consequently on 30 October 1882 a burgher commando under the leadership of Gen Piet Joubert set out from Middelburg and invested the Ndzundza mountain stronghold near Namashaxelo. In reality this was little more than a series of caves where Nyabele and his people had thought of making a tactical retreat. No records exist of the exact number of Boers engaged in this campaign but, judging from General Joubert's letters, it appears that no more than 1000 to 2000 men were ever in the field at any one time.

Certainly the Boers do not appear to have had much stomach for the fight, leading Joubert to complain to the Volksraad that the burghers "seemed to prefer looting cattle for their own account". After a long campaign of nearly nine months, the Ndzundza, starved and dynamited into submission, capitulated and handed Mampuru, bound hand and foot, over to the Boers. Both Mampuru and Nyabele were taken prisoner to Pretoria where they were tried for insurrection and sentenced to death. The British, who had previously supported Mampuru's claims to the Pedi leadership, attempted to intercede on their behalf with the ZAR, but their efforts were only partially successful, for while Nyabele's sentence was commuted to life imprisonment, Mampuru was hanged in Pretoria Prison on 22 November 1883.

At the same time the Volksraad declared the Ndzundza ancestral lands to be forfeit to the ZAR Government, which then proceeded to parcel them out to members of Joubert's commando. The surviving Ndzundza were indentured for five years as labourers to the farmers in the district, thus effectively scattering them and breaking their power as a tribe forever.

In retrospect the ZAR Government might appear to have acted in a somewhat precipitous manner in what was, after all, an internecine squabble which did not present them with an immediate threat. However, for the ZAR the question of Pedi succession was a sensitive one which needs to be read in conjunction with political conditions prevailing in the Transvaal at the time. Since the establishment of the Transvaal Republic in 1852, the region had remained in an almost constant state of anarchy.

The wars against the Tswana in 1852 and 1858, and against Makapane in 1854; the rise of separate Boer republics at Utrecht (1854), Lydenburg (1856), and Zoutpansberg (1857); the establishment of a Boer revolutionary government in the Waterberg in 1860 and the four years of civil war which followed it; the Swazi attack upon the Ndebele, instigated by the Boers in 1864; the war against the Venda, the Boer retreat from the Zoutpansberg and the destruction of Schoemansdal by the Venda in 1867; and the disastrous war upon the Pedi in 1877, all depleted its resources, and by the time the British annexed the Transvaal on 12 April 1877 its government was bankrupt and on the point of collapse.

Boer independence from British rule was only regained after a brief series of battles in 1881, and thus it was to be expected that any challenge made against the newly-established government of the ZAR would be met with harsh and immediate force. The newly-elected

Volksraad must have been understandably anxious to avoid a return to conditions prevailing in the Transvaal five years previously while, at the same time, serving notice to British and Black alike that it was determined to maintain the independence it had regained only the previous year.

Msiza settlement at Hartbeesfontein

During the years of Nyabele's imprisonment, some of his family and personal advisers were allowed to settle on the white-owned farm of Hartbeesfontein, located between Wonderboom and Derdepoort north of Pretoria, in order to be near him. These were lands previously occupied by the Ndebele prior to their move to Namashaxelo, but which had since been annexed by the Transvaal government for white occupation. Shortly before the outbreak of the South African War of 1899-1902 Nyabele was granted a pardon. However he was not allowed to return to Namashaxelo but rejoined his followers at Hartbeesfontein where he is believed to have died in about 1903.

He was succeeded by Mfene, the second son of his eldest brother Soqaleni, who had preceded Nyabele as chief of the Ndzundza. Mfene is reported to have lived at Hartbeestfontein for a few years before moving with the bulk of his family and followers to a site on the upper reaches of the Wilge River, known as Weltevrede, near Vaalfontein.

Mfene was followed by his son Maysha and, when he died in about 1951, he was succeeded by Mabusa David Mahlangu who continues to reside at Weltevrede.

The contingent of Nyabele's immediate family and followers included Kgalabi (also given as Umghalabi) Msiza whose family, the Msiza, traditionally enjoyed the high status of "shield-bearers to the Ndzundza king". He settled at Hartbeesfontein where, in time, he became the patriarch of a substantial extended family. His first wife, Usmeshe, raised a family which included six sons, while his second, Nomatombeni Dina Mahlangu, bore him another five. The number of daughters in the family is not known. Nomatombeni was the daughter of Nyabele and his wife Sibiya, and probably met and married Kgalabi at Hartbeesfontein.

When Mfene and the majority of his retinue relocated to Weltevrede, for reasons which are not clear the Msiza family chose to remain at Hartbeesfontein where they continued to farm their lands. By all accounts they flourished, and by the 1950s Kgalabi's extended family settlement included the homesteads of nine sons, three of whom had two wives each. The settlement also included the home of Zondiwe Jacob Bhuda, who had married Umdundwana Amy Msiza, daughter of

Kgalabi's brother, who probably joined the Hartbeesfontein community after Mfene's group had departed for Weltevrede.

The date of Kgalabi's death is not known, but can probably be assumed to have taken place during the 1930s or the early 1940s Leadership of the Hartbeesfontein community thereafter devolved upon Hlangane Speelman Msiza, his oldest son by his senior wife, Usmeshe. In time Hlangane became known to his white neighbours as Cornelius Speelman.

The resettlement of the Msiza at ODI

Despite the fact that the Msiza family continued to live and farm at Hartbeesfontein, the property remained in the ownership of a family called Wolmarans. At that time it was a common arrangement for black farmers living on "white" land to exchange their labour for a small piece of ground where they could build their homesteads and plant a small crop. However, they had no title to this land, no tenure or work contracts, and could lose their homes at the whim of the white owner. By all accounts Wolmarans was considered to have been "a good man", and the Msiza remained at Hartbeesfontein for nearly sixty years. When Wolmarans died in about 1952, his son-in-law found it expedient to sell the property to the developers of the new

Wonderboom airport, and the Msiza were forced to find new homes elsewhere.

By this time the Ndebele had begun to decorate the walls of their homesteads with a variety of polychromatic designs, and at an early stage the practice had come to the notice of architects, artists and anthropologists. Among them was Prof AL Meiring, Head of the School of Architecture at Pretoria University. He appears to have begun visiting the Msiza at Hartbeesfontein early in the 1950s, and at one stage he and his students drew up a detailed record of the settlement. When the family found itself in the position of being evicted from their homes, Meiring interceded on their behalf with the authorities and made it possible for them to be resettled in an area known as Klipgat, in the district of Odi, located some 50km north of Pretoria. Meiring further facilitated the move by obtaining grants of building materials for the family, most particularly timber and thatch.

By 1953 the Msiza, under the leadership of Hlangane, had rebuilt their homes at Odi and their old homestead at Hartbeesfontein had been demolished. They were joined in the move by members of the Bhuda and Skosana families, who had married Msiza women and now belonged to the extended Msiza family group. One additional family, also called Msiza but not directly related to the Kgalabi line, also made its home at Odi. Initially this move involved some 21 nuclear families, but as at least three of the men were polygamous, the number of families units was probably closer to eighteen.

In the 1960s Hlangane Msiza died, and leadership of what had by now grown into a village passed on to his brothers. Today this rests with Hlangane's last surviving brother, Maselwane Msiza who, despite his advanced age, still enjoys good health and clear thinking. His memories of events at Hartbeesfontein, and thereafter, form the basis for much of what has been related here.

Although never given an official name, the village began to appear on road signs and various large-scale maps as either KwaMapoch, Speelman's Kraal, or simply as The Ndebele Village. Its residents however, prefer the term KwaMsiza, which translates to "the place of the Msiza".

By the 1960s the village had become a popular stopping point for tourists, a factor assisted by the South African Tourist Board who placed it upon its itineraries of local attractions, and its residents had begun to supplement their income through the manufacture and sale of beaded artifacts. It did not take long for Msiza women to develop a name for themselves as excellent bead workers, and their handiwork was to inspire similar developments among other Ndebele families in the region. Articles about the Msiza and their colourful, polychromatic habitat began to be carried by numerous journals, both local and overseas, thus increasing their fame as a community of artists.

Unfortunately the agricultural lands allocated to the Msiza were neither suitable for planting, nor were they large enough to sustain the growing community. As a result many of its menfolk, as well as some of the women, were forced to enter the migrant labour market. In most cases this took them away from home for eleven months of the year, and although their income helped to sustain their families, their absence from home for such long periods had a negative effect upon the quality of life now enjoyed in the village. Most of the responsibility for the raising of children now fell upon the women, and although this was not unique to the Msiza in the context of the Apartheid society which developed in South Africa during the 1950s and 1960s, the Ndebele reaction to this oppression had some unique and interesting results. This was most marked in such areas as wall decoration and codes of ceremonial female dress.

During the 1960s and early 1970s the people of KwaMsiza were to enjoy a period of relative stability and prosperity. Assisted by grants of thatching grass and paint from the South African Tourist Board, they continued to maintain their homes to a standard which continued to attract visitors to their homes and clients for their beadwork. Work was also available, and although absent from their families as migrant workers, the men were able to earn money on a constant basis. However, by the mid-1970s the nation-wide drought had begun to have a serious effect upon the already meager crops they could grow. Their economic well-being was aggravated after June 1976 when a national student revolt made international headlines and heralded the beginning of a more intensive resistance against white Apartheid government. Although the district was not directly involved in the events of 1976, many whites were deterred from entering black residential areas by both the threat of violence as well as the ominous presence of South African security forces, and the number of visitors to the village dropped dramatically. Added to this was the fact that many men, previously employed in the migrant labour market, lost their jobs and returned home to their families, thus increasing their financial burden.

Pedi

(baPedi – People and sePedi – Language)
The four major ethnic divisions among Black South Africans are the Nguni, Sotho-Tswana, Shangaan-Tsonga and Venda. Together the Nguni and Sotho account for the largest percentage of the total Black

population. The major Sotho groups are the South Sotho (Basotho), the West Sotho (Tswana), and the North Sotho, which includes the Pedi people.

Language, culture and beliefs:

Language: The difference between Northern Sotho and Sepedi

Northern Sotho, or Sesotho sa Leboa, is one of South Africa's 11 official languages, and consists of up to 30 different dialects, one of which is Pedi. Much confusion surrounds this term, as Sepedi, the language spoken by the Pedi people, which has been often referred to as Northern Sotho, which is incorrect.

The confusion between Northern Sotho and Pedi probably arises from the fact that the missionaries who developed the orthography for Northern Sotho mainly had contact with the Pedi people. However, Northern Sotho or Sesotho sa Leboa, is not the same as Sepedi. Sepedi is the language of the Pedi people, also known as the BaPedi.

Sepedi is closely related to the official language of Setswana or Tswana, and the dialect of Setlokwa and the similar Sotho language, Sesotho sa Borwa, or Southern Sotho. Sepedi is mainly spoken in the northern parts of South Africa, including the provinces of Mpumalanga, Limpopo, Gauteng and the North West province.

Settlements

Early Pedi settlements were divided into kgoro (pl. dikgoro), which are groups centred around agnatic [from the father's side] family clusters. According to research by Peter Delius, members of a kgoro were not always strictly agnatic, and according to circumstances other non-relatives were known to be accepted into a kgoro.

A kgoro consisted of a group huts built around a central area which served as meeting-place, cattle byre, graveyard and ancestral shrine. These were ranked in order of seniority. Each wife of a polygynous marriage had her own round thatched hut, which was joined to other huts by a series of open-air enclosures called lapa encircled by mud walls.

Older boys and girls would be housed in separate huts, which are referred to as 'age sets', and were an important element of Pedi social hierarchy.

Subsistence and economy

Early Pedi settlements were subsistence farmers, and grew sorghum, pumpkins and legumes, which were cultivated by women on fields allocated to them when they married. Women hoed and weeded; did pottery and built and decorated huts with mud; made sleeping mats and baskets; ground grain, cooked, brewed, and collected water and wood.

Men did some work in fields at peak times; hunted and herded; did woodwork, prepared hides, and were metal workers and smiths. Most major tasks were done communally by matsema (work-parties).

Cattle also played an important role in Pedi society, as it was not only a source of food, but also an important status symbol, and used as bohadi or bridewealth payments.

Labour division shifted significantly after the introduction of the animal-drawn plough, and maize (mielies), and due to the effects of labour migration.

Young men left home to work as migrant labourers in regimental groups, in order to satisfy the paramount's need for firearms and ammunition and to assist individual household income. Migrant labour was also a prominent feature of life under apartheid, as population increases in homelands or reserves, and land degradation, meant that men would have to leave home to work for wages to support their families, who could not survive on subsistence farming alone.

Delius also points out that many young men were drawn to migrant labour because it enabled them to buy cattle in order to marry.

It said that despite long absences due to migrant labour, men still remained committed to their fields. This required ploughing during their time of leave, a job that was also handed over to professionals or tractor owners.

Women were then left to perform all the other agricultural tasks, while the men, who were subject to restrictions on their lives to being wage-labourers, resisted direct involvement in cattle-keeping and agriculture. They resisted so much in fact, that a rebellion took place, which was quelled in the 1950s. Later on, families would continue to practice cultivation and keep livestock, which was more a way of gaining retirement security in a rural social system than a means of household subsistence.

In the early 1960s, about 48% of the male population was absent at any given time. From the 1930s to the 1960s, most Pedi men would spend some time working on a nearby White farm. This would be followed by employment on the mines or domestic service, and later, especially in more recent years, to employment in factories or industry.

Recently, female wages have also begun, but are generally more rare and sporadic. Some of these women work on farms for short periods or as domestic workers in the towns of the Witwatersrand since the 1960s.

Religion

The Pedi practice ancestral worship (phasa) which involves animal sacrifice and the offering of beer to the 'shades' on both the mother's and father's side. Another important ritual figure was the kgadi (father's older sister). The position of ngaka (diviner) was traditionally inherited via patrilineal lines, but this position is now inherited by a woman from her paternal grandfather or great-grandfather.

The position of diviner is said to be manifested through illness and violent spirit (malopo) possession. The only cure for these ailments is to train as a diviner. Apparently, there has been an increase in the number diviners recently, many of whom are believed to be driven only by a desire for material gain. The chief also played the role of rain-maker for his subjects.

In today's Sotho society, Christianity in various forms is accepted, as many Sotho-speaking groups were converted by Christian missionaries. Lesotho has a large percentage of Catholics, but also has Protestant denominations.

There are also a number of independent churches that combine elements of African traditional religion with Christianity. These churches emphasize healing and the Holy Spirit. One of the most well known of these churches is the Zion Christian Church (ZCC), which was founded by two Pedi brothers. The ZCC has an enormous following and attracts followers from all over South Africa. Each spring there is a "Passover" meeting at the churches' headquarters in the Northern Province, in Moria, which is attended by thousands of people.

Arts

Important elements of Pedi arts include metal-smithing, which was a common practice in the Pedi area and surrounds. Other art forms made by the Pedi include beadwork, pottery, house-building and painting, as well as woodwork and the making of drums.

Pedi music (mmino wa setso: traditional music, lit. music of origin) is made up of a six-note scale. This kind of music was formerly played on a plucked reed instrument called dipela, but its musicians now use trade-store instruments such as the Jew's harp, and the German autoharp (harepa), which are now regarded as characteristically Pedi.

The height of Pedi musical expression is said to be the kiba genre, which has surpassed its rural roots and has become a migrant style. In its men's version it is played an ensemble, each member playing an aluminium end-blown pipe of a different pitch (naka, pl. dinaka).

Together this ensemble produces a descending melody with harmonies.

In the women's version they sing songs (koÅ¡a, pl dikoÅ¡a) and improvise on older lyrics. This is a development of earlier female genres which have recently been included within the definition of kiba. a group of women sings songs (koÅ¡a, pl dikoÅ¡a) in which Both male and female groups are accompanied by an ensemble of drums (meropa), which were previously wooden but are now made of oil-drums and milk-urns.

Land tenure

The pre-colonial system of communal or tribal tenure which was similar to that practised throughout the southern African region was cemented, but subtly altered, by the colonial administration. A man was granted land by the chief for each of his wives; and unused land was reallocated by the chief, rather than being inherited within families.

Overpopulation resulted from the government's relocation policies, and the system was then modified. A household's fields, and its residential plot, are now inherited, ideally by the youngest married son.

Christian Pedi communities who owned freehold farms were removed to the reserve without compensation, but since 1994 South Africa many have now reoccupied their land or are preparing to do so, under restitution legislation. The few Pedi who still live as labour tenants on White farms have been promised some security of tenure by land reform legislation.

Kinship

Kgoro, or subdivisions of villages and chiefdoms, were made up of a collection of kinsmen with related males at the centre. These kgoro were also jural and kinship units and acceptance into a particular kgoro was up to the kgoro-head's authority, and was not only determined by relations. Royal or chiefly dikgoro were often faced with subdivision, as sons competed for authority.

The eldest son of a household within a polygynous family would be set to inherit his mother's property, including cattle, and was assigned the task of custodian to the other children in the household. However, due to a decline in cattle-keeping and increases in land-shortage, this system of inheritance has now altered so that the last-born inherits primarily land.

Marriage

In traditional Pedi society, marriage was patrilocal, and polygyny was practised by those with a higher social status, including chiefs. Marriage to a cousin was preferred in the ruling dynasty, as this ensured a degree of political integration and control. This is because the two-sets of in-laws were already connected, and the bohadi (bridewealth) could then be used for further bohadi payments within the ruling house.

Initiation

The life of both girls and boys was differentiated by important rituals, such as initiation. Boys called baÅ¡emane and later maÅ¡oboro) would spend their youth herding cattle at remote outposts with their peers and others from older age-sets.

Initiation would also include circumcision at koma (initiation school) which would be held about once every five years. This initiation process socialised youths into groups or regiments called mephato which would bear the leader's name, and whose members would then be loyal to each other for their lifetimes. These groups or regiments would often travel together to work on farms or on the mines.

Girls attended their own koma and were divided into their own regiments, a process that usually took place two years after the boy's school. Initiation is still practised today, and provides a substantial income to the chiefs who licence it for a fee or. In recent years private entrepreneurs have also established initiation schools, outside the chiefs' jurisdiction.

Origins

Monarchy

According to historians, Pedi society has it's origins in the northern Transvaal. The Pedi began as a confederation of small chiefdoms sometime before the 17th century, and over time, strong Pedi chiefs claimed land from smaller chiefdoms, and dominated trade routes from the interior to the coast. Historians also credit the Pedi with the first monarchy in the region, but their rule was marked by occasional military defeat and population disruption.

The Maroteng and their symbolic animal noko (porcupine) were an offshoot of Tswana-speaking Kgatla. In about 1650 settled in the area to the south of the Steelpoort River and here, over several generations, linguistic and cultural homogeneity developed to a certain degree. Only in the last half of the 18th century did they broaden their influence over the region, establishing the Pedi paramountcy by bringing powerful neighbouring chiefdoms under their control.

During migrations in and around this area, groups of people from diverse origins began to concentrate themselves around dikgoro (s. kgoro) or ruling nuclear groups. They identified themselves through symbolic allegiances to totemic animals such as tau (lion), kolobe (pig) and kwena (crocodile).

The Pedi area, or heartland, is known as Sekhukhuneland, and is situated between the Olifants and Steelpoort Rivers, which are also known as the Lepelle and the Tubatse. The area is named after Sekhukhune I, the son of Sekwati.

Before this, the Pedi polity under Thulare (c. 1790-1820) was made up of land that stretched from present-day Rustenburg to the lowveld in the west and as far south as the Vaal river. Pedi power, at its height during Thulare's reign (about 1790-1820) was undermined during the period of the Difaqane, by Ndwandwe invaders from the south-east. A period of dislocation followed, after which the polity was re-stabilised under Thulare's son Sekwati.

Sekwati succeeded Thulare as paramount chief of the Pedi in the northern Transvaal (Limpopo) and was frequently in conflict with the Matabele under Mzilikazi, and plundered by the Zulu and the Swazi. Sekwati was also engaged in numerous negotiations and struggles for control over land and labour with the Afrikaans-speaking farmers (Boers) who had since settled in the region.

These disputes over land occurred after the founding of Ohrigstad in 1845, but after the town was incorporated into the Transvaal Republic in 1857 and the Republic of Lydenburg was formed, an agreement was reached that the Steelpoort River was the border between the Pedi and the Republic.

The Pedi were well equipped to defend themselves though, as Sekwati and his heir, Sekhukhune I were able to procure firearms, mostly through migrant labour to the Kimberley diamond fields and as far as Port Elizabeth. The Pedi paramountcy's power was also cemented by the fact that chiefs of subordinate villages, or kgoro, take their principal wives from the ruling house. This system of cousin marriage resulted in the perpetuation of marriage links between the ruling house and the subordinate groups, and involved the payment of inflated bohadi or bride wealth, mostly in the form of cattle, to the Maroteng house.

Sekhukune I succeeded his father in 1861, and repelled an attack against the Swazi. At the time, there were also border disputes with the Transvaal, which lead to the formation of Burgersfort, which was manned by volunteers from Lydenburg. By the 1870s, the Pedi were one of three alternative sources of regional authority, alongside the Swazi and the ZAR (Zuid-Afrikaansche Republiek).

However, tension increased after Sekhukhune refused to pay taxes to the Transvaal government, and the Transvaal declared war in May 1876. It became known as the Sekhukhune War, the outcome of which was that the Transvaal commando's attack failed. After this, volunteers nevertheless continued to devastate Sekhukhune's land and provoke unrest, to the point where peace terms were met in 1877.

However, unrest continued, and this became a justification for the British annexing the Transvaal in April 1877, under Sir Theophilus Shepstone. Following the annexation, the British also declared war on Sekhukhune I under Sir Garnet Wolseley, and defeated him in 1879. Sekhukhune was then imprisoned in Pretoria, but later released after the first South African War, when the Transvaal regained independence.

However, soon after his release Sekhukhune was murdered by his half-brother Mampuru, and because his heir had been killed in the war and his grandson, Sekhukhune was too young to rule, one of his other half-brothers, Kgoloko assumed power as regent.

In 1885, an area of 1000 square metres was set aside for the Pedi, known as Geluk's Location, created by the Transvaal Republic's Native Location Commission. Later, according to apartheid segregation policy, the Pedi would be assigned the homeland of Lebowa.

Lobedu

The smaller Lobedu population makes up another subgroup among the Northern Sotho. The Lobedu are closely related to the Shona population, the largest ethnic group in Zimbabwe, but the Lobedu are classified among the Sotho primarily because of linguistic similarities. The Lobedu were studied extensively by the early twentieth-century anthropologist J.D. Krige, who described the unique magical powers attributed to a Lobedu female authority figure, known to outsiders as the rain queen.

Missionary Settlements

In 1858, Alexander Merensky, a missionary from the Berlin Missionary Society, was instructed to open a missionary station in Swaziland. After failed negotiations with the Swazi, Merensky was then granted consent to build three mission stations in Sekwatis territory, namely Gerlachshoop, Khalatloloe and Petametsane, west of the Leolo Mountains.

However, when Sekwati was succeeded by Sekhukhune I, Christian converts were persecuted, and the missionary station moved to BotÅ¡habelo (the place of refuge), near Middleburg, south-west of the Pedi area.

From here, several groups of converts later left to purchase land and found their own independent communities – including Doornkop and Boomplaats.

Merenksy, who was also played an ethnographic role in the recording of Pedi customs and life at this time, was also involved in mediating between Sekhukhune I and the Transvaal in 1877.

Here Christian Pedi continued living until they were forcibly removed into the Pedi reserve called Lebowa during the 1960s-70s in the interests of "ethnic consolidation".

Social and Cultural Life

The Pedi lived in huts, which were round in shape and known as rondawels. Rondawels were made out of clay mixed with "boloko"(cow dung) in order to strengthen it. The roofing of the rondawels was made from a particular grass called "loala" which was strong and long, and they would pack the grass in bangles and roof the houses.

Traditional Pedi food consisted of; thophi (a meal which is made from maize mixed with a fruit called lerotse), morogo wa dikgopana (spinach cooked and given a round shape and left to dry up in the sun). Bogobe ba mabele, samp and maswi (milk), masonja (mopane worms) is also eaten as well as vegetables and fruits like milo and machilo.In Pedi culture the chief would wear clothes made out of wild animal skin such as Leopard and Lion to show leadership and he was from the ruling house (moshate). Ordinary people wore clothes made out of domestic animal skin such as goats, sheep and cows. However, the Pedi have changed their mode of dressing because of the present trends in fashion. There are many spoken dialects of Sepedi but only one written language. The Pedi are known for storytelling. The stories are usually told in the evenings but nowadays radio and TV have replaced them.War Tactics:

It could hardly be said that the Pedi were a warlike tribe, and it is difficult to determine whether they ever had the courage to fight a battle with a rival tribe. Pedi custom was to send men to the opposing tribe, for doctoring or of selling bead work but, in truth, they were spies who reported upon an opportunity for waging attack on the kraal. The chief would then summon all the men of his tribe to assemble with their weapons, which mainly consisted of assegais and battle-axes. The men were aware of the need to bring food supplies for the duration of the journey. It did not take long to for the men to assemble, and the whole of the Pedi army would set off in the opposite direction to their destination which was kept secret from the main following until the second night, when suddenly the course would be changed and they would rush on to the targeted kraal.The attack was made stealthily and no prisoners were taken, except the women and children. In most cases the attacks were effective and a great deal of bloodshed resulted. Unlike the Zulus and the Matabele, to whom the art of war and military strategy was a science and military discipline was a way of life; the military organization of the Pedi was very primitive. Each man in a Pedi tribe provided for himself and followed his own ideas as to what he should do. Tactics were formulated by the chief in council, and the execution of the tactics was assigned to the chief's brother, who took on the task of active command over the tribesmen. All the cattle looted were handed to the man in command, who made sure that a third was slaughtered, a third was sent to the chief's kraal and the remaining third to be handed back to the men who had looted the opposing tribe. Women and children were regarded as loot and divided among the followers of the chief.

Belief System

The Pedi believe in ancestors and gods, they believe that through ancestors they can talk to gods about their needs. They also believe that when the time is right young men and women should go to initiation school. They also reckoned that anyone who violates how things are done concerning culture and their tradition is to be taken away from the village.

Pedi Rituals: When it comes to marriage the elders would choose the spouse for their son or daughter. If the parents knew their child liked someone in the village they would go to that family and introduce themselves, to discuss the future nuptials. And thereafter arrangements would be made on how the two people would meet. A decision would then be made by the girl's parents as to how many cows or money will be paid as Bogadi, then the 2 may be together. If a man died, an unmarried younger brother would marry the widow, in order to support the family and take care of the children.

The mother usually gave birth at her family home and after she returned to her husband's home, her family would contribute meat and beer for the subsequent feast. As a tribute to the status of the new mother, her husband would build her a homestead. When a baby was born to the chief the villagers have to go to the royal house (moshate), give presents to the child, and wish the baby well. After a few days there would be an announcement from the chief's servants that a ceremonial party would be held whereby the villagers would sing and rejoice for the newborn baby with food and drink that is traditionally prepared. When a person dies they bury him / her after 7 days so that they could have enough time to arrange everything including informing the friends, relatives and all the people who need to know about the death of that particular person. This was in order to give them time to be able to attend to the funeral. The day before the person is going to be buried they will cover him / her with cow skin. Everybody will then get a chance to see that person for the last time (go tlhoboga), and the following day he / she will be buried.

Music and Dance:

Songs were also part of Pedi culture. During hard labour the Pedi would sing together to finish the job quickly. One particular song was about killing a Lion to become a man. The act of killing a Lion is very unusual and no longer practised. Actually it was so unusual that if a boy managed, he would get high status and the ultimate prize - to marry the chief's daughter.

The Pedi today

In the 1950s a Pedi migrant workers' organisation (Sebatakgomo) tried to cast out chiefs, headmen and others who accepted Bantu authorities and rural betterment programmes. In 1958 a major protest took place in Sekhukhuneland in which those who sought to defend the chieftainship were challenged by the new forces. The Northern Sotho homeland of Lebowa was proclaimed a 'self-governing' territory in 1972, with a population of almost 2 million. Economic problems plagued the poverty-stricken homeland, however, and the people were not unified. Lebowa's chief minister, Cedric Phatudi, struggled to maintain control over the increasingly disgruntled homeland population during the early 1980s, his death in 1985 opened new factional splits and occasioned calls for a new homeland government. Homeland politics were complicated by the demands of several ethnic minorities within Lebowa to have their land transferred to the jurisdiction of another homeland. At the same time, government efforts to consolidate homeland territory forced the transfer of several small regions of land into Lebowa. Conflict broke out again in 1986 in what had by then become the Bantustan of Lebowa.

San

The San

The San, the first people in South Africa

The earliest hunter-gatherers in southern Africa were the San people. The San were also known as 'Bushmen', a term used by the European Colonists that is now considered derogatory. The San populated South Africa long before the arrival of the Bantu-speaking nations, and thousands of years before the arrival of Europeans.

Language, culture and religion:

San languages, characterised by implosive consonants or 'clicks', belonged to a totally different language family from those of the Bantu speakers. Broadly speaking, they are two different and identifiable languages, namely the Khoikhoi and San. Many dialects have evolved from these, including /Xam, N?Âi, !Xu, Khwe and Khomani. NÁʃ mÁʃÂi, previously called Hottentot, is the most populous and widespread of the Khoikhoi and San languages.

Very little is known about the different dialects of South Africa's San people, as most of these beautiful, ancient languages were never recorded. Fortunately, the /Xam dialect, which is spoken by the San, was recorded almost in its entirety, thanks to the work of a German linguist, Dr WHI Bleek.

/Xam speakers originally occupied a large part of western South Africa, but by 1850, only a few hundred /Xam speakers lived in remote parts of the Northern Cape. Today, the language is no longer exists, but survives in 12 000 pages of hand-written testimony taken down word-for-word from some of the last /Xam speakers in the 1860s and 1870s. These pages record not just the /Xam language, but also their myths, beliefs and rituals. A comprehensive /Xam dictionary was produced by Dr Bleek at the time, but was only published years later (DF Bleek: 1956).

South Africa's motto, written on the SA coat of arms is a /Xam phrase: !ke e: /xarra //ke, literally meaning: diverse people unite.

Archaeological evidence determines a way of life:

Archaeological evidence shows that South Africa was part of a large region, including North and East Africa, in which modern humans first evolved and lived. Hundreds of thousands of generations of Stone Age hunter-gatherers populated the South African landscape for nearly two million years, yet for most of that time we know nothing of their names, language, memories beliefs, wars or alliances.

The San are the best model we have for the hunter-gatherer lifestyle that saw so many generations through the Stone Age, and it is tempting to say that the history of the later Stone Age is the history of the San. This can only be done at a very broad level of generalization, but evidence does points to a 'San' history.

For example, human skeletal remains buried mainly in the last 10 000 years are broadly similar to those of the ninetieth and twentieth century San people. The 'toolkits' of the more modern San people are similar to those artefacts found and dated back to later Stone Age hunter-gatherers. Finally, the uniqueness and diversity of the San 'click' languages suggest very ancient roots that possibly date back into the middle Stone Age period.

There are three kinds of evidence that give us clues as to the development of the early South African hunter-gatherers and later the San. These consist of human bone fragments and art artefacts (like beadwork and rock art) as well as the examination of the places where these people lived, and the food remains that they left behind.

Rock art by the late Stone Age hunter-gatherers can be found in the form of paintings or engravings in almost every district in South Africa. There is no comprehensive list of all sites, and many have not been recorded, but it is estimated that there are at least 20 000 to 30 000 sites and well over a million individual images. Although many are not well preserved, collectively they represent a remarkable record of the beliefs and cultural practices of the people who made them. Most were created by San hunter-gatherers, but Khoikhoi herders and Iron Age farmers added to the collection.

Khoikhoi herders who brought sheep and cattle into this part of South Africa within the last 2 000 years were probably responsible for the most recent phase of painting, in which the paint was applied with a finger instead of a brush. The colours are mostly monochrome and the subject matter is frequently non-representational patterns with symbolic meaning. As the Khoikhoi settled on the land formerly occupied by hunter-gatherers, the San gradually stopped painting as their numbers and cultural activities declined.

The San have a rich oral history and have passed stories down from generation to generation. The oldest rock paintings they created are in Namibia and have been radiocarbon-dated to be 26 000 years old. The San rock art gives us clues about their social and belief systems.

One of the most significant pieces of Rock art found in South Africa was found on Linton Farm in the Eastern Cape. The panel was removed from the farm in 1917 and taken to the South African Museum in Cape Town. It is known as the Linton panel, and an image from this panel was used in the new South African Coat of Arms.

Eighty-three years in museum care, protected from the elements, has made the Linton panel one of the best preserved of all pieces of South

African rock art. In 1995, the panel featured as one of the premiere attractions in the international exhibition, "Africa: the Art of a Continent".

The figure embodies the spirit of the African Renaissance. When European nations began their Renaissance, they turned to the classical age of Greece and Rome when art and architecture had reached its zenith. San rock art is one of the great archaeological wonders of the world, and is a mirror which reflects the glories of the African past.

Our knowledge of South African San texts (especially the 12 000 pages of testimony collected by Dr Bleek), combined with the study of the rituals and beliefs of San people still living in the Kalahari, allows us to understand many of the paintings in the Linton panel. The panel shows people capturing a power the /Xam called !Gi. The San sought and used this power for the benefit of their community ,as it allowed for the healing of the sick and for the healing of divisions within society. San rock art was believed to be rich in this special power.

A dying way of life:

The ability of Later Stone Age hunter-gatherers to sustain themselves was seriously challenged at least three times in the past 2 000 years. Firstly, this occurred with the southward migration of the Khoikhoi herders into the western half of the country. Although they appear to have developed a symbiotic relationship with the hunter-gatherers, they converted individuals to herding, and therefore weakened hunter-gatherer social cohesion.

Secondly, hunter-gatherers were challenged in the north and east of South Africa, as Iron Age farmers (Nguni and later Sotho nations) had settled in the summer rainfall regions within the last 1 800 years to grow crops and tend their stock. They also lived alongside hunter-gatherers, particularly in the Drakensberg region, and developed a working relationship with them. However, they became more and more powerful in terms of population size and land ownership. Finally, the death knell came with the arrival of European colonists whose commandos with guns and horses decimated the hunter-gatherers within two centuries. Some of this history is reflected in the rock art of the later Stone Age.

In the 1950s, several thousand San people were still hunting large game with poisoned arrows and gathering plant food in the Kalahari Desert in Namibia. One group, the !Kung, lived in an area called Nyae Nyae (pronounced ny ny, rhyming with high), near the border between Namibia and Botswana.

The !Kung were able to continue their ancient way of life largely because they lived in an area that was very difficult to reach. A stretch of land of about 200 km, waterless for most of the year, lay between the closest farms and the Nyae Nyae area. Travelling across this area, even in trucks, was difficult. Vehicles would get stuck in the sand, tyres would get punctured or the seeds of the tall, dry grasses would clog up their radiators causing them to boil. These factors helped to protect the !Kung way of life from outside influences until about thirty years ago.

In the 1960s, the Department of Nature Conservation began to take over large sections of the traditional hunting lands of the Kalahari San for game and nature reserves. A law passed in 1970 meant that the !Kung lost 90% of their traditional land in Nyae Nyae. Today, they have hardly any land on which to hunt and gather.

Social & Cultural life:

The San have no formal authority figure or chief, but govern themselves by group consensus. Disputes are resolved through lengthy discussions where all involved have a chance to make their thoughts heard until some agreement is reached. Certain individuals may assume leadership in specific spheres in which they excel, such as hunting or healing rituals, but they cannot achieve positions of general influence or power. White colonists found this very confusing when they tried to establish treaties with the San.Leadership among the San is kept for those who have lived within that group for a long time, who have achieved a respectable age, and good character. San are largely egalitarian, sharing such things as meat and tobacco. Land is usually owned by a group, and rights to land are usually inherited bilaterally. Kinship bonds provide the basic framework for political models. Membership in a group is determined by residency. As long as a person lives on the land of his group he maintains his membership. It is possible to hunt on land not owned by the group, but permission must be obtained from the owners

The San will eat anything available, both animal and vegetable. Their selection of food ranges from antelope, Zebra, porcupine, wild hare, Lion, Giraffe, fish, insects, tortoise, flying ants, snakes (venomous and non-venomous), Hyena, eggs and wild honey. The meat is boiled or roasted on a fire. The San are not wasteful and every part of the animal is used. The hides are tanned for blankets and the bones are cracked for the marrow. Water is hard to come by, as the San are constantly on the move. Usually during the dry season, these migrants collect their moisture by scraping and squeezing roots. If they are out hunting or travelling, they would dig holes in the sand to find water. They also carry water in an ostrich eggshell.

Hunting Methods:

The San are excellent hunters. Although they do a fair amount of trapping, the best method of hunting is with bow and arrow. The San arrow does not kill the animal straight away. It is the deadly poison, which eventually causes the death. In the case of small antelope such as Duiker or Steenbok, a couple of hours may elapse before death. For larger antelope, this could be 7 to 12 hours. For large game, such as Giraffe it could take as long as 3 days. Today the San make the poison from the larvae of a small beetle but will also use poison from plants, such as the euphorbia, and snake venom.A caterpillar, reddish yellow in colour and about three-quarters of an inch long, called ka or ngwa is also used. The poison is boiled repeatedly until it looks like red currant jelly. It is then allowed to cool and ready to be smeared on the arrows. The poison is highly toxic and is greatly feared by the San themselves; the arrow points are therefore reversed so that the poison is safely contained within the reed collar. It is also never smeared on the point but just below it - thus preventing fatal accidents.The poison is neuro toxic and does not contaminate the whole animal.

The spot where the arrow strikes is cut out and thrown away, but the rest of the meat is fit to eat. The effect of the poison is not instantaneous, and the hunters frequently have to track the animal for a few days. The San also dug pitfalls near the larger rivers where the game came to drink. The pitfalls were large and deep, narrowing like a funnel towards the bottom, in the centre of which was planted a sharp stake. These pitfalls were cleverly covered with branches, which resulted in the animals walking over the pit and falling onto the stake.When catching small animals such as hares, guinea fowls, Steenbok or Duiker, traps made of twisted gut or fibre from plants were used. These had a running noose that strangled the animal when it stepped into the snare to collect the food that had been placed inside it. Another way of capturing animals was to wait at Aardvark holes. Aardvark holes are used by small buck as a resting place to escape the midday sun.

The hunter waited patiently behind the hole until the animal left. When this happened, it was be firmly pinned and hit on the head with a Kerrie (club). The San are intelligent trackers and know the habits of their prey. On discovering where a herd has gathered, they immediately test the direction and force of the wind by throwing a handful of dust into the air. If the ground is bare and open, he will crawl on his belly, sometimes holding a small bush in front of him. Hunters carry a skin bag slung around one shoulder, containing personal belongings, poison, medicine, flywhisks and additional arrows. They may also carry a club to throw at and stun small game, a long probing stick to extract hares from their burrows or a stick to dig out Aardvark or Warthog.Hunting is a team effort and the man whose arrow killed the animal has the right to distribute the meat to the tribe members and visitors who, after hearing about the kill, would arrive soon afterwards to share in the feast.

According to San tradition, they were welcome to share the meal and would, in the future, have to respond in the same way. However, plant foods, gathered by the womenfolk, are not shared but eaten by the woman's immediate family. The San make use of over 100 edible species of plant. While the men hunt, the women, who are experts in foraging for edible mushrooms, bulbs, berries and melons, gather food for the family. Children stay at home to be watched over by those remaining in camp, but nursing children are carried on these gathering trips, adding to the load the women must carry.Gender roles are not jealously guarded in the San society. Women sometimes assist in the hunt and the men sometimes help gather plant foods.

Rock Art:

Until recently, most amateur and professional anthropologists looked at a rock painting of the San and believed that they could decipher it without any problems. The pieces that they did not understand were passed off as crude art or that the artist had too much to drink or smoke. This has been found not to be the case, and their work is recognised as holding deep spiritual and religious meaning. Contrary to popular belief, these paintings and engravings of strange human figures and animals, especially the Eland (a species of antelope), did not depict every day life but had a deeper religious and symbolic meaning.

When shaman (medicine men) painted an Eland, they did not just pay respect to a sacred animal; they also harnessed its essence (N!um). By putting paint to rock, they would be able to open portals to the spirit world. San rock paintings are found in rocky areas of the KwaZulu-Natal, Eastern Cape and the Western Cape provinces. The San mainly used red, ranging from orange to brown, white, black and yellow in their paintings. Blue and green were never used. Red was derived from haematite (red ochre), and yellow from limonite (yellow ochre).Manganese oxide and charcoal were used for black; white, which does not preserve well, was probably obtained from bird droppings or kaolin.

The blood of an Eland, an animal of great religious and symbolic significance, was often mixed into the colour pigments. Another striking feature of the rock art is the embodiment of action and speed. Human figures are stylized and depicted as having long strides and the animals are either galloping or leaping, or, more subtly, flicking a tail or twisting a neck. Most of the paintings have an underlying spiritual theme and are believed to have been representations of religious ceremonies and rituals.

San Belief System:

The San belief system generally observes the supremacy of one powerful god, while at the same time recognizing the presence of lesser gods along with their wives and children. Homage is also paid to the spirits of the deceased. Among some San, it is believed that working the soil is contrary to the world order established by the god. Some groups also revere the moon. The most important spiritual being to the southern San was /Kaggen, the trickster-deity. He created many things, and appears in numerous myths where he can be foolish or wise, tiresome or helpful.The word '/Kaggen' can be translated as 'mantis', this led to the belief that the San worshipped the praying mantis. However, /Kaggen is not always a praying mantis, as the mantis is only one of his manifestations. He can also turn into an Eland, a hare, a snake or a vulture - he can assume many forms. When he is not in one of his animal forms, /Kaggen lives his life as an ordinary San.

San Rituals:

The Eland is their most spiritual animal and appears in 4 rituals:

- ✓ Boys' first kill

- ✓ Girls' puberty

- ✓ Marriage

- ✓ Trance dance

A ritual is held where the boy is told how to track an Eland and how the Eland will fall once shot with an arrow. The boy will become an adult when he kills his first large antelope, preferably an Eland. Once caught, the Eland is skinned and the fat from the animal's throat and collarbone is made into a broth. In the girls' puberty rituals, a young girl is isolated in her hut at her first menstruation. The women of the tribe perform the Eland Bull Dance where they imitate the mating behaviour of the Eland cows.

A man will play the part of the Eland bull, usually with horns on his head. This ritual will keep the girl beautiful, free from hunger and thirst and peaceful. As part of the marriage ritual, the man gives the fat from the Elands' heart to the girls' parents. At a later stage, the girl is anointed with Eland fat. In the trance dance, the Eland is considered the most potent of all animals, and the shamans aspire to possess Eland potency. The San believed that the Eland was /Kaggen's favourite animal. San people have vast oral traditions, and many of their tales include stories about the gods that serve to educate listeners about what is considered moral San behaviour.

Music & Dance:

Of prime importance in all San groups is a ritual dance that serves to heal the group. The great 'medicine or healing dance' and the rain dance were rituals in which everyone participated. During these dances, the women usually sat around a central fire as they sang and clapped their hands. The men then first danced around the women in a clockwise direction and then vice versa. As the dance increased in intensity, the dancers reached trance-like, altered, states of consciousness and were transported into the spirit realm where they could plead for the souls of the sick.

These trance dances are depicted in the rock art left behind by the San. The shamanic figures are often painted in strange 'bending forward' postures. Shamans or 'medicine men' explained later that they adopted this posture during their trance dances because they experienced a great deal of pain when the 'potency' started boiling in their stomachs and their stomach muscles started contracting. They also often experienced spontaneous nosebleeds at this time. These nosebleeds are depicted in the many rock paintings of trance dances. As other groups invaded the territory of the San and influenced their way of life, the pictures of soldiers, wagons and horses served to record historical events.

The Kalahari San held similar beliefs and revered a greater and a lesser god, the first associated with life and the rising sun, and the latter with illness and death. The shamans, who went into trances and altered states of existence during ritual dances, thus acquired access to the lesser god who caused illness. Birth, death, gender, rain and weather were all believed to have supernatural significance, for example, people acquired good or bad rain-bringing abilities at birth and this ability was reactivated when the person died.Another shared belief was the fact that, when the world was first created, animals and people were indistinguishable. People had not yet acquired manners and culture and only after the second creation, were they separated from the animals and educated in a separate social code. Most San believed that upon death, the soul went back to the great god's house in the sky. Dead people could, however, still influence the living and, when a medicine man died, the people were very concerned lest his spirit become a danger to the living.

Life of the San today:

Today, the San suffer from a perception that their lifestyle is 'primitive' and that they need to be made to live like the majority cattle-herding tribes. Specific problems vary according to where they live. In South Africa, for example, the !Khomani now have most of their land rights recognised, but many other San tribes have no land rights at all. Few modern San are able to continue as hunter-gatherers, and most live at the very bottom of the social scale, in unacceptable conditions of poverty, leading to alcoholism, violence, prostitution, disease and despair. The last of the hunter-gatherers were forcibly evicted from the Central Kalahari Game Reserve as recently as April 2002, by the Botswana government to make way for diamond mines.

A court case is currently in existence to help the San claim their land. The official reason was to provide them with services such as schools and medical services, and to bring them into modern society. In fact, few of these services have materialized, and the San have been confined to bleak encampments in a hostile environment. The San are a friendly, creative, and peaceful people, who never developed any weapons of war, and have lived in harmony with their natural environment for at least 20 000 years. Properly restored to their ancestral lands, and reintegrated into the game reserves of southern Africa, San communities could become self-sustaining. The hardiness of the San allowed them to survive their changed fortunes and the harsh conditions of the Kalahari Desert in which they are now mostly concentrated.

Today, the small group that remains has adopted many strategies for political, economic and social survival. The San retain many of their ancient practices but have made certain compromises to modern living. The westernised myths regarding the San have caused considerable damage. They portray the San as simple, childlike people without a problem in the world. This could not be further from the truth.Due to absorption but mostly extinction, the San may soon cease to exist as a separate people. Unfortunately, they may soon only be viewed in national museums. Their traditions, beliefs and culture may soon only be found in historical journals

The Cape Malay

The 'Cape Malay' community is rich in culture and religious traditions that have played a major role in shaping the history and diversity of Cape Town.

Origins

The exploration of the African continent in the fifteenth century and the colonization of South East Asia in the sixteenth century by European powers led to the enslavement of millions of Afro-Asian peoples. European powers exploited ethnic differences by employing the divide and rule tactic and used military conquest to subdue resistance by the local inhabitants. As a consequence Europeans exercised almost total control over virtually of these two continents. One of the reasons linked to colonial expansion in Africa and Asia was trade and the search for new markets. The need for labour to sustain trade created a massive international slave trade which led to the involuntary migration of large numbers of Africans and Asians to different parts of the world. For instance it is estimated that Africa alone supplied some 20 million slaves over three centuries in order to satisfy the American demand for labour.

Although slavery and the slave trade flourished off the coast of West and East Africa, Southern Africa remained largely untouched. This changed after the VOC established their presence at the Cape. Dutch settlers at the Cape of Good Hope arrived in 1652 when Jan van Riebeeck came to the Cape to establish a trading post and supply fort for trading vessels plying the Europe-East Indies route. The Dutch settlers were given land and required to produce enough food to meet the supply needs of the VOC ships and the settlement. Settlers or 'free burgers' that were granted land demanded cheap labour in order for them to produce enough supplies. The VOC used this as an opportunity to import political exiles from the East Indies to work as slaves in the Cape Colony.

The VOC which colonised portions of South East Asia and practiced slavery introduced the system to the Cape. Those people that opposed the colonization and occupation of their lands by the Dutch were taken as political prisoners or shipped to exile at the Cape of Good Hope as slaves. The first slaves arrived in the latter half of the seventeenth century with the initial load coming from Africa. Their ship was captured by the Dutch from a Portuguese ship destined for Brazil. However, the majority of slaves were gradually brought to the Cape from the Dutch East Indies in Asia by the Dutch. A large majority of those being brought were Muslims, were captured and sent into exile from colonies such as Madagascar, India, Ceylon and the Dutch East Indies (known as Indonesia today). Other immigrants were from Philippines, Japan, Macau, Malacca, West Indies, Brazil and possibly New Guinea.

The origins of this migration can be traced to early in the sixteenth century when, at the end of Indonesia's Majapahit Kingdom, European military penetration and anti-Islamic persecution caused resistance which was crushed by the Dutch. This led to many opponents of the Dutch being exiled to the Cape of Good Hope in southern Africa, which was also occupied by them. Some were also brought or captured from English, French and Portuguese ships. Included in this group were the Malay servants of the Dutch officials who were on their way back to the Netherlands from the East. The main group of African immigrant's came from East Africa, Madagascar and West Africa. Many of these people were skilled artisans, such as silversmiths, milliners, cobblers, singers, masons and tailors. This group came to be known collectively as the 'Cape Malay,' despite their diverse origins as far afield as East Africa and Malaysia.

Anyone who opposed the colonization of their countries would be taken as political prisoners or exiles. It was one such group of people that were brought to the Cape of Good Hope. The first of these migrants arrived in the latter half of the seventeenth century, mainly from colonies in Africa and Asia that were occupied by the Dutch and the British.

The large majority being Muslims, were captured and sent into exile from colonies such as Madagascar, India, Ceylon and the Dutch East Indies (Indonesia as we know it today). Some immigrants were from Philippines, Japan, Macau, Malacca, West Indies, Brazil and possibly New Guinea. Some were also brought or captured from English, French and Portuguese ships. Included in this group were the Malay servants of the Dutch officials who were on their way back to the Netherlands from the East.

The main group of African immigrant's came from East Africa, Madagascar and West Africa.

The origins of this migration can be traced to early in the sixteenth century when, at the end of Indonesia's Majapahit Kingdom, European military penetration and anti-Islamic persecution caused resistance which was crushed by the Dutch. This led to many opponents of the Dutch being exiled to the Cape of Good Hope in southern Africa, which was also occupied by them.

The first Dutch settlers at the Cape of Good Hope arrived in 1652, when Jan van Riebeeck came to the Cape to establish a trading post and supply fort for trading vessels plying the Europe-East Indies route.

The Dutch required labour and utilised the opportunity to import political exiles from the East Indies as slaves. Many of these people were skilled artisans, such as silversmiths, milliners, cobblers, singers, masons and tailors. This group came to be known collectively as the 'Cape Malay,' despite their diverse origins as far afield as East Africa and Malaysia.

Orang Cayen - Men of Repute

Sheikh Yusuf

One prominent figure among the exiles, or Orang Cayen (Men of Repute), who resisted the Dutch occupation of the East Indies, was Sheikh Yusuf al-taj alkhalwatial-Maqasari. Credited with having brought Islam to South Africa, Sheikh Yusuf was born in 1626 in Goa on the island of Celebes (today known as Sulawesi). Sheikh Yusuf was the son of Makassarese nobility, and the nephew of King Bissu of Goa.

Sheikh Yusuf spent several years studying Arabic and traditional religious sciences in Mecca. He eventually returned to Banten, West Java, where he taught the Islamic doctrine of "Khalwatiyyah", which he had learned during his years spent in Mecca.

He eventually joined forces with Sultan Ageng in his fight against the Dutch attempts to gain complete control of the Sultanates in the East Indies. In 1683, Sheikh Yusuf was captured and exiled to Ceylon and eventually brought to the Cape of Good Hope. On 2 April 1694, Sheikh Yusuf, together with 49 other Muslim exiles from the East Indies arrived at the Cape aboard the ship "de Voetboeg."

Sheikh Yusuf, his family and followers were sent to Zandvliet farm at the mouth of the Eerste River, just outside Cape Town, to prevent his influence on the Islamic slave population. It is ironical that this farm had belonged to a minister of the Dutch Reformed Church, the Rev Petrus Kalden. Under the leadership of Sheikh Yusuf, who was 68 years of age at the time, the group at Zandvliet established one of the first elementary structures of a Muslim community. Dutch attempts to isolate them failed as Zandvliet became a gathering spot for Muslims and a rallying point for runaway slaves, and other exiles from the East. This farm area is now known as Macassar. As Sheikh Yusuf's influence and spiritual teachings spread widely amongst the slaves at the Cape, they came to represent one of the first areas of resistance to colonisation at the Cape.

Repeated calls from the people and the King of Goa to have Sheikh Yusuf released and sent home were refused by the Dutch. In 1698, the Batavian Council issued a definite refusal to even consider the request and a year later on 23 May 1699, Sheikh Yusuf died. He was buried on a hill overlooking Macassar. A tomb constructed there in his memory is among the 25 Islamic shrines or kramats that encircle Cape Town. Sheikh Yusuf's remains were brought to Makassar (Ujung Pandang of today) in 1705 and interred in a tomb located in Katangka Village, bordering on the Goa regency. The teachings of Sheihk Yusuf established a sound Muslim community at the Cape. His insightful approach and understanding of the religion still continues today.

Tuan Guru

Another prominent person was Imam Abdulla Kadi Abdus Salaam, or as he is now referred to as 'Tuan Guru' (which means Master Teacher) who was born in Tidore in Tinnate Islands of Indonesia in 1712 and became a Prince of this Muslim Sultanate. Tuan Guru was captured in 1780 by the Dutch for allegedly conspiring with the English and was sent as a religious prisoner to Robben Island. He was a keen academic and whilst he was a prisoner, he completed a book on Islamic law titled 'Ma'rifant al-Islam wa al-Iman' which explained practices of the Ash'ari creed of Sunnism and stressed the acceptance of the faith of Allah's will in the world. This creed particularly suited the experiences of exiles and slaves. It also included discussions on scared cures and amulates, thus combining philosophical teaching with the more mystical faith that had developed amongst Cape Town's underclass. Tuan Guru's teaching and philosophy provided the basis of Cape Islam until mid-to-late nineteenth century. During this time there was a shift from a hidden and mystical form of Islam to a more open and public practice of the faith.

After his release in 1792, he set up a madrassah at his house in Dorp Street and by 1797; he was given permission to convert a warehouse in Dorp Street into the Auwal Mosque. It is said that Tuan Guru transcribed the Koran from memory as there were no copies at the Cape in his day. Later, when copies were brought to the Cape, it was found that his version contained very few errors. A kramat was erected to his honour on Robben Island.

The Holy circle of Kramats (tombs)

From the tomb of Sheikh Yusuf, a series of kramats stretch in a rough circle around the Peninsula. Besides Sheikh Yusuf's shrine, these embrace the tombs on Robben Island, Signal Hill, Oude Kraal and Constantia.

The tombs of Signal Hill Cemetary belong to the three Tuans that are buried there: Guru,Syed and Nurman.

The second Tuan was known by the nickname 'Oupa Skapie'.

The third Tuan may have come from Arabia but very little information is available on him.

It is believed that the kramat at Oude Kraal is that of Nureel Mobein who escaped from Robben Island. (*No solid evidence to prove this is available; we can only rely on tradition.*)

The question of identity

The terms Malay and Muslim are often used as synonyms but strictly speaking Malay stands for that section of the local Muslim community in which the descendents of Eastern Malays are to be found.

The question of identity has also been raised in South Africa, particularly by the minority communities as they formed part of the marginalised sectors of the community, oppressed masses and neglected groups. During the apartheid period, many rejected the racial policies of the White minority regime and never identified themselves as South Africans.

According to the Population Registration Act of 1950, South Africans were divided into four distinct categories: Whites, Indians, African and Coloureds. The Coloured group was further sub-divided into 'Cape Malay', Khoisan, other Coloureds, Bastards, et al. Researchers have pointed out that the Coloured identity has never been seen as an identity in its own right because it has been negatively defined and did not fit the classificatory schemes created by the apartheid politicians.

Most of the Western Cape's Muslims were put into the 'Cape Malay' category and thus they inherited the negative connotations that were attached to this category of people. According to Muhammed Haron from the University of Botswana, researchers such as Robert CH Shell use the term 'Cape Malay' as many of them came from the east, although the term 'Indonesian' would have been fairly accurate. Shell explains that the Cape Muslims came to be known as 'Cape Malay' because Malay was the lingua franca of the Indonesian Archipelago and the language was widely spoken at the Cape during and prior to the nineteenth century.

This term remained employable by those who trekked to other parts of the country and neighbouring countries as well. There were occasions, however in the nineteenth and twentieth centuries that the 'Cape Malays' were regarded as respectable people who did not drink and were hard working and reliable. This differed from the other 'Coloured' groups and the 'Malays' seem to have maintained those distinctions mainly because of their religious and cultural traditions. During the traumatic socio-political and economic crises of the 1970's and 1980's, the 'Coloureds' and their sub-categories appended the term 'so-called' to their ethnic identities, this was a clear reflection of them experiencing an identity crisis. It was during these times that the younger generation of the 'Cape Malay' group preferred to be called South African Muslims instead of South African 'Cape Malays', thus employing the religious label instead of the ethnic one.

Achmat Davis believed that the term 'Cape Malay' was unacceptable as it teemed with racist prejudice. This belief was held by Davis at the time when the general Muslim populace sympathised and supported the internal and external liberation movements against apartheid. In the socio-political context of the time, the masses rejected all ethnic labels imposed by the state. However, Davids later accepted the term 'Cape Malay' and used it interchangeably with term 'Cape Muslim'. There seems to be continuous conflict between those who are in favour of the term and those who opposed it.

Today, the 'Cape Malay' form the larger section of the local Muslims who can roughly be divided into two groups; the Cape Malay's whose home language is Afrikaans and the Indians, who speak English and their own vernacular languages. For both groups, Arabic is the language of their religion but for the Cape Malay, it is supplemented by Afrikaans.

The 'Cape Malay' community generally speak mostly Afrikaans but also English, or local dialects of the two. Although they no longer speak the Malay languages and other languages which their ancestors used, various Malay words and phrases can still be heard in Cape Town today.

Areas of Settlement

When the 'Malay' exiles and slaves arrived at the Cape, they settled at Gallows Hill which was later known as De Waterkant (today this form part of Green Point). The Gallowsteen or execution gallows was constructed here and slaves who protested against the cruelty of the

Dutch were executed here. With the introduction of the Group Areas Act in 1950, all the families at Waterkant were forcibly moved to the outer areas of Cape Town.

Bo-Kaap

Other Muslims slaves were scattered across the town before emancipation, although a number of Muslim free Blacks were beginning to concentrate in the area on the slopes of Lion's Rump later known as the Bo-Kaap. Other slaves settled in the Devils Peak area which already had an established community.

By 1840, Cape Town established its first municipality and the cluster of houses from Hanover Street to Lowry Street then became known as District 12. By 1849, the population rose considerably and the area expanded rapidly due to the emancipation of a number of slaves. Many 'Malays' settled here, a number of whom lived in the area above the open field in the vicinity of Muir Street.

This area was originally known as Kanaladorp. This name was a mixture of Maleyu and Dutch and mostly likely referred to people assisting each other, a community spirit: the literal meaning being 'if you please'. Early Kanaladorp was not only ethnically mixed but socially as well. In 1867, Cape Town was divided in six districts and

Kanaladorp became the sixth district, henceforth people referred to the area as District Six.

District Six

District Six had a large concentration of 'Malay' people. This area was mainly a working class area. Living conditions varied enormously as you could find one family in a detached house while other house could contain up to 16 people in a single room.

Toilets were usually in the backyards and baths had to be taken in the kitchen in huge tubs. However, due to overcrowding, the area quickly turned into a slum area. In spite of this, there existed a joyous spirit and common bond amongst the inhabitants who had been living there for years. Sadly, in 1966, under the Group Areas Act, District Six was declared a 'White' area as government regarded the region as a health hazard to the city. As a result many 'Malay' people were moved along with others to the Cape Flats area.

Culture and traditions

The 'Cape Malays' have preserved their cultural identity and Islamic creed.

Language

The Afrikaans language evolved as a language of its own through a simplification of Dutch in order for the slaves to be able to communicate with the Dutch and amongst each other. Educated Muslims were the first to write texts in Afrikaans.

The 'Cape Malay' community generally speak mostly Afrikaans. English is used to a lesser extent, or local dialects of the two can also be heard. Although they no longer speak the Malay languages and other languages which their ancestors used, various Malay words and phrases can still be heard in Cape Town today for example: 'terima kasin' which is the Malay equivalent for 'thank you', and 'salmaat djalen' which is 'good journey to you'.

Home life
The 'Cape Malay' people follow Islamic principles of living. On Thursday nights, Malay people burn incense sticks (niang) in preparation for Friday.

Fasts and feasts
A feast to which relatives are invited to is known as a 'merang' and it is usually held to celebrate a special occasion. The following fasts and feasts are observed by all Malay people.

Moulood'n-Nabi (Birthday of the Prophet- PBUH)
This day is celebrated on the 12th day of Rabi-ul-Auwal. The prayers

for this day are certain recitations from the Quran and songs that are sung in harmony. Women practice at least three months in advance for this ceremony. The Malay community celebrate by going to the mosque on the Saturday afternoon where they cut up orange leaves which are then dipped into sweet smelling oils and tied up in sachets. This is known as 'rampies sny'. At the evening prayer, at the mosque, sweetmeats are served and the little sachets of scented orange leaves are given out as gifts. This tradition which is believed to be of Indonesian origin gave the slaves a link to their ancestral home. The purpose of this ceremony is to send praises (salawat) to the Prophet (PBUH).

Mir'raj

This is a celebration in memory of the Prophet's (PBUH) journey in one night from Mecca to Majid Al-Aqsa (known as Jerusalem) and then to the 7th Heavens and back.

Roa

Roa is on the 15th of the Islamic month of Shabaan and is a feast of purification.

Ramadaan

The most important fast in the Muslim calendar is the month in which the revelation of the Koran began. All Muslims must observe it, except those who are ill, travellers, the old, women who are pregnant, and children under the age of puberty. The Muslim year is determined by the sighting of the moon and the fast commences by the new moon in the beginning of the ninth Islamic month. The Islamic months consists of 29 or 30 days, depending on the sighting of the moon and the Islamic New Year starts on the month of Muharram and ends with the month Thul-Haj. The 'Malay' community refer to this fast as 'poewasa'.

The most important day in the fast is the 27th night which is described in the Koran as the 'night of power'. It is said in the Koran that during this holy night the sins of the faithful are forgiven and the angels and souls of Heaven come down to earth to perform many miracles.

The Malay people clean their houses in preparation for this night and candles are lit (kers-opsteek).

Lebaran Ramadaan (Eid-al-Fitr)

The sighting of the new moon again brings the holy month of Ramadaan to an end. This day is celebrated by all Muslims around the world. The day begins early as the men go to the mosque for a special Eid prayer or 'Eid salaah'. Thereafter in their new clothes, families visit and greet each other. Gifts are exchanged and elaborate food is prepared for the day.

Lebaran Hadji (Eid-ul- Adha)

This feast is known throughout the Muslim world as Eid-al-Adha. It is held after the hajj pilgrimage. A sheep is sacrificed by families who can afford to do so and shared with the poor.

Malay Food

Popular amongst Malay people are dishes such as bredie, frikkadels, denningvleis, sabananvleis, pinangkerrie, sosastie and bobotie and although the 'Malay 'people have changed their diet, these dishes still seem popular at the Cape.

Stews, roasts and baked vegetables still form part of the Malay diet but the food is very peppery and spicy.

Contact with the Dutch colonists left it's mark as many old Cape dishes such as 'melktert' and 'koeksisters' are still to be found in Malay homes.

Weddings

When a Malay man decides to get married, he asks his father to approach his prospective father in law and should they agree to the man's hand in marriage then the couple become engaged or 'lambaar'. A time is fixed for the wedding and money 'maskowi' is paid to the bride to be. This money, which varies in amount, is according to the groom's means and is paid to the priest who hands It over to the bride.

On the wedding day, the bride wears a 'medora' or headdress which is reminiscent of the golden ballets of Bali, and receives her guests in her first wedding dress. She does not attend the wedding ceremony which takes place at the mosque but is represented by her father or another male member of her family. A feast takes place usually for lunch at the bride family. Thereafter she changes her dress and joins the groom's family for supper. At the end of the evening the bride is taken to her new home by her in laws or 'khujadi's'.

Early Malay dress

Early Malays wore a distinctive Mulsim style of dress: a toedang conical 'kopdoek' and the 'kaparring' wooden sandals, these originated in South-East Asia. Imams and others of higher status wore turbans.

The Khalifa
The Khalifa is a 'Malay' sword dance which takes place on the 11th day of Rabi-al-Agier in honour of Abdul Kadir Beker, a follower of the Prophet (PBHU). Its original religious implications have been modified with the result that the Khalifah now amounts to a skilful exhibition of sword play. Some Imams condone it as symbolic of the power of flesh

over steel through faith, while others disapprove. The players, invariably state that they are aided by prayer.

Although the Khalifah or chalifah is the name of the central person conducting the ceremony, in South Africa it is often used for the ceremony itself. The Malay people used the word 'ratiep' for the actual performance. It is said that if one attends a Khalifa performance, one becomes conscious of the hypnotic effect which the rebanas have in conjunction with the rhythmic chanting, the incense and the general performance. For the rest skilful sword play explains unusual dance.

New Year's Carnival

Each year on the 2nd of January or 'Tweede Nuwe Jaar' the Bo Kaap celebrates a big street party, known as the 'Coon Carnival' in the centre of town. Originally, this was introduced by the Muslim slaves who celebrated their only day off work in the whole year. Nowadays men, woman and children march from the Grand Parade to the Green Point stadium. Plans for the parade are started a year in advance for the troupes that take part. Elaborate costumes are designed and sewn by 'Malay' tailors and are kept a secret until the day of the carnival as troupes are judged by their costumes, singing and dancing. Clad in colourful, shiny suits, hats and sun umbrellas, in true Rio Carnival style, the spirit and vitality of the Cape Minstrels continue to fascinate both tourists and locals alike. The 'Coon Carnival' has become one of the biggest events on the Cape Town calendar.

Music

This cultural group developed a characteristic type of Cape Malay music. One particular interesting secular folk song type, of Dutch origin, is termed the *nederlandslied*. The language and musical style of this genre reflects the history of South African slavery. Often, it is described and perceived as 'sad' and 'emotional' in content and context. The nederlandslied shows the influence of the Arabesque (ornamented) style of singing which is unique in South Africa, Africa and probably in the world.

Remnants of the old 'Malay' culture is still to be found in Cape Town today as a thriving Cape Malay community lends character to the mother city of South Africa. Cape Malay architecture, food (such as bobotie and yellow rice, samoosas, rotis, etc.), tailor shops, mosques and the warmth and hospitality of the Malay people continue to attract tourists in abundance to the mother city. Malaysians and Indonesians are starting to visit Cape Town in increasing numbers to experience this cultural link for themselves.

Tsonga

The Tsonga are a diverse people, generally including the Shangaan, Thonga, Tonga, and several smaller ethnic groups. Together they numbered about 1.5 million people in South Africa in the mid-1990s, with some 4.5 million individuals in southern Mozambique and Zimbabwe.

Historical Background

The first Tsonga-speakers to enter the former Transvaal probably did so during the 18th Century. They were essentially traders who followed rivers inland, where they bartered cloth and beads for ivory, copper and salt. The Shangaan tribe came into being when King Shaka of the Zulu, sent Soshangane (Manukosi) to conquer the Tsonga people in the area of present-day southern Mozambique, during the Mfecane upheaval of the 19th Century.

Soshangane found a fertile place inhabited by scattered communities of peace-loving people, and he decided to make it his home rather than return to Shaka. The Shangaan were a mixture of Nguni (a language group which includes Swazi, Zulu and Xhosa), and Tsonga speakers (Ronga, Ndzawu, Shona, Chopi tribes), which Soshangane conquered and subjugated.

Soshangane insisted that Nguni customs be adopted, and that the Tsonga learn the Zulu language. Young Tsonga men were assigned to the army as 'mabulandlela' (those who open the road). Soshangane also imposed Shaka's military system of dominion and taught the people the Zulu ways of fighting. Soshangane's army overran the Portuguese settlements in Mozambique, at Delagoa Bay, Inhambane and Sena, and during the next few years, he established the Nguni kingdom of Kwa Gaza, which he named after his grandfather, Gaza. The Gaza Kingdom comprised parts of what are now southeastern Zimbabwe, as well as extending from the Save River down to the southern part of Mozambique, covering parts of the current provinces of Sofala, Manica, Inhambane, Gaza and Maputo, and neighbouring parts of South Africa.

Another army, under the command of Dingane and Mhlangana, was sent by Shaka to deal with Soshangane, but the army suffered great hardship because of hunger and malaria, and Soshangane had no difficulty, towards the end of 1828, in driving them off. During the whole of this turbulent period, from 1830 onwards, groups of Tsonga speakers moved southwards and defeated smaller groups living in northern Natal; others moved westwards into the Transvaal, where they settled in an arc stretching from the Soutpansberg in the north, to Nelspruit and Barberton areas in the southeast, with isolated groups reaching as far westwards as Rustenburg.

After the death of Soshangane in 1856, his sons fought over the chieftainship. Soshangane had left the throne to Mzila, but Mawewe felt that he should be chief. Mawewe attacked Mzila and his followers, causing them to leave Mozambique and flee to the Soutpansberg Mountains in the Transvaal.Mzila stayed with João Albasini at Luonde. Albasini, who had been appointed by the Portuguese Vice-Consul to the Zuid Afrikaansche Republiek (ZAR) in 1858, employed many of the Tsonga men as 'indhuna' (headman), and defenders of his fort-like home at the foot of the Piesangkop near the modern town of Makhado (formerly known as Louis Trichardt). Aided by Albasini and traders at Lourenço Marques, Mzila gained the upper hand, returning and defeating Mawewe in 1862.

Mawewe fled to Swaziland, where he sought the help of King Mswati I, finally settling in northern Swaziland on the border with Gazaland. Ngungunyane, who succeeded Mzila, was defeated by the Portuguese in 1895, which caused the collapse of the Gaza kingdom.The Tsonga came to João Albasini for protection and they considered Jiwawa (the Tsonga version of his name) as their chief. Between 1864 and 1867, the Tsonga were involved in the battles between Paul Kruger's commandos and the Venda chief Makhato. For their services they were rewarded some land near the town of Schoemansdal. This area became known as the 'Knobneusen Location', because of the habit the Tsonga had acquired of tattooing the nose. Later the Shangaan people fled to the Lowveld after the Portuguese conquered them. The descendants of both Tsonga and Shangaan lived together in the area and a great deal of interaction occurred between the two groups.

The Tsonga-Shangaan homeland, Gazankulu, was carved out of northern Transvaal Province during the 1960s and was granted self-governing status in 1973. The homeland economy depended largely on gold and on a small manufacturing sector. Only an estimated 500,000 people - less than half the Tsonga-Shangaan population of South Africa - ever lived there. Many others joined the throngs of township residents around urban centres, especially Johannesburg and Pretoria. Traditionally, each Tsonga family had its own 'village' composed of a few houses and a kraal, surrounded by the fields and grazing areas. From 1964, the government started resettling the people in rural villages of 200 to 400 families. These resettlements brought tremendous changes in the life of the people, some for the better (roads, schools, water, etc), some for the worse (scattering of the enlarged family, lack of privacy, problems with cattle, distance form the fields, and so forth).

Social and Cultural Life

Traditionally, the Tsonga lived mainly by fishing for subsistence. A few goats and chickens were raised, and crop cultivation was important. Their tsetse fly-infested coastal lowland habitat made cattle raising an uncommon practice. By the 18th Century, most Tsonga were organised into several small and independent chiefdoms in which inheritance by brothers, rather than sons, was a defining feature of the social system, a practice common in many Central African societies but rare among other South African groups. Compared with common western family structures, the traditional social structures of the Tsonga tribes are quite complex.

The smallest social unit that can be determined is the 'nuclear family', consisting of a woman with her own hut and cooking area, her husband and their children. For Tsonga men, the possibility of having more than one wife exists. In cases of polygamy, 'extended families' came about, consisting of a group of nuclear families, headed by the same man. When the sons of an extended family married, a settlement, or muti came about, consisting of a man, his wives, their unmarried children and the families of their married sons. Traditionally, these settlements appeared as circular living areas, surrounded by wooden walls. Inside this circle, various huts and cooking spots were built.

Large thatched conical roofs typify the style of their homes. Wide beaded necklaces and heavy metal bracelets are also popular. Within the Tsonga community, different social units exist. Aside from the family units mentioned above, lineages or nyimba exist, consisting of persons who can prove they descend from the same ancestors. The various lineages can be grouped into clans or xivongo, consisting of all persons, who descend from the same ancestor. In present times, the Tsonga community structure is based on tribal relationships. A tribe is a group of people, which recognises the authority from one tribal chief or hosi, and is living in a specific tribal area, or tiko ra hosi.

Belief System

Whilst generally in BaNtu culture, and specifically in Shangaan-Tsonga culture, a Supreme Being is acknowledged, far more relevant are the powers of ancestors who are believed to have considerable effects on the lives of their descendants. The ancestors appear mainly in dreams, but sometimes manifest themselves as spirits. Some spirits or ancestors are believed to live in certain sacred places where ancient chiefs have been buried. Each clan has several of these burial grounds. The ancestors are propitiated by prayers and offerings, which range from beer to animal sacrifices. The Sangoma, on behalf of the community, makes offerings in times of trouble or in cases of illness, and on special occasions.

Care is taken to please the ancestors, as restless ancestors can cause trouble. Children are named after their ancestors to ensure continuity in the family. According to the Tsonga, there exists a strong relationship between the creation (ntumbuloko) and a supernatural power called Tilo. Tilo refers to a vaguely described superior being, who created mankind, but it also refers to the heavens, being the home of this creature. The Tsonga believed that man had a physical (mmiri) and a spiritual body with two added attributes, the moya and the ndzuti. The moya is associated with the spirit, enters the body at birth, and leaves at death to join the ancestors. The ndzuti was associated with the person's shadow and reflected human characteristics. At death, in the spirit world, it left the body.

This meant that the spirit was attached with the individual and human characteristics of that person. Inherent in this concept is not only the belief in life after death but also that the dead retain very strong links with the living. Passing over into the spirit world is an important stage in the life of a Tsonga.The members of the family performed a welcoming ceremony to help ease the passage of the dead person into the spirit world. The death of a member of the family also caused all the other members in the homestead to become unclean and they all had to go through ritual cleansing ceremonies.

These ceremonies were performed at different times of the day over the next few months. During religious ceremonies, the family gathered at a special area to pay homage to the ancestral spirits. Food and drink was offered to the ancestors to thank them for providing for the people. Face scarring in Shangaan-Tsonga culture had its origin in deterring Arab slave traders but it is now considered a sign of beauty. The transition from youth to adulthood is a truly warlike affair, where patterns are burnt into the skin.

It is important to know that in the traditional Tsonga worldview, society is an overall unity, consisting of both the living and the dead. Aside from their belief in serving the ancestral spirits, there exists also a strong belief in magic, which can be used for evil purposes (vuloyi), practised by evil servants (valoyi), with the purpose to harm the community. Good spirits brought rain and caused good things to happen, and evil spirits, controlled by sorcerers, caused great harm to the community.

Illness or persistent bad luck usually indicated the presence of baloyi (evil spirits) but occasional illness was accepted as part of everyday life.However, if the illness was serious or the cycle of bad luck persisted, a cure had to be found through divination. Traditional healers (tin'anga) consulted the ancestral spirits by "throwing" the bones (tinholo), shells or other artefacts and were thus able to determine the cause of the bad luck and suggest ways in which to get rid of the cause. Traditional healers, also combine magic and the knowledge of medicinal plants (mirhi) in favour of the community.

Shangaan Music and Dance

In the Shangaan-Tsonga tradition, the storyteller is the grandmother or elder woman of the family who is the respected transmitter of the old stories. The old woman, called Garingani, or narrator, begins her storytelling by saying "Garingani, n'wana wa Garingani!" - "I am Narrator, daughter of Narrator!" after which the crowd cheers "Garingani". The crowd chants her name after each line of the story.With a love for music, the Shangaan-Tsonga people have developed a number of musical instruments. The 'fayi' - a small, stubby wooden flute that produces a breathless, raspy, but haunting sound, and is often played by young herd boys. The 'xitende', is a long thin bow tied on each end by a taut leather thong or wire - which runs across a gourd. This was often used to alleviate boredom on long journeys. The Shangaan-Tsonga is well known for their mine dances, carried out to the beat of drums and horns and wide variety of musical instruments such as the mbila. Shangaan-Tsonga male dancers performed the muchongolo dance, which celebrated the role of women in society, war victories and ritual ceremonies.

Life of the Shangaan Today

A living monument to the Shangaan culture was officially opened on 23 February 1999 near Hazyview, Mpumalanga. The Cultural Village aims to enhance tourism and contribute to job creation, foreign currency earnings and economic development. Today, the Shangaan live in areas mainly between the Kruger National Park and the Drakensberg Mountains, in South Africa's Mpumalanga and Northern Provinces. Their sister tribe, the Tsongas, inhabit most of southern Mozambique.

Tswana

(seTswana [language], baTswana [people])
The four major ethnic divisions among Black South Africans are the Nguni, Sotho-Tswana, Shangaan-Tsonga and Venda. Together the Nguni and Sotho account for the largest percentage of the total Black population. The major Sotho groups are the South Sotho (Basuto and Sotho), the West Sotho (Tswana), and the North Sotho (Pedi).

Language, culture and beliefs:

About 4 million Tswana people live in southern Africa; 3 million in South Africa and 1 million in the nation of Botswana. In South Africa, many Tswana live in the area that formed the numerous segments of the former homeland, Bophuthatswana, as well as neighboring areas of the North-West Province and the Northern Cape. Tswana people are also found in most urban areas throughout South Africa.

Tswana culture, social organizations, ceremonies, language and religious beliefs are similar to that of the other two Sotho groups (Pedi and Sotho), although some Tswana chiefdoms were more highly stratified than those of other Sotho groups or the Nguni. Tswana culture is often distinguished for its complex legal system, involving a hierarchy of courts and mediators, and harsh punishments for those found guilty of crimes.

Like many neighboring Nguni peoples, the Sotho traditionally relied on a combination of livestock raising and crop cultivation for subsistence. Most Sotho people were traditionally herders of cattle, goats, and sheep, and cultivators of grains and tobacco. In addition, Sotho were skilled craftsmen, renowned for their metalworking, leatherworking, and wood and ivory carving.

Also like the Nguni, most Sotho people lived in small chiefdoms, in which status was determined in part by relationship to the chief. Unlike the Nguni, Sotho homesteads were grouped together into villages, with economic responsibilities generally shared among village residents. Villages were divided into wards, or residential areas, often occupied by members of more than one patrilineal descent group.

The village chief (a hereditary position) generally appointed ward leaders, whose residences were clustered around the chief's residence. Sotho villages sometimes grew into large towns of several thousand people. Farmland was usually outside the village, not adjacent to the homestead. This village organization may have enabled the Sotho villagers to defend themselves more effectively than they could have with dispersed households, and it probably facilitated control over ward leaders and subjects by the chief and his family.

The cattle kraal is central to most traditional Tswana villages and is the focus of life. Tswana believe in voluntary work on behalf of other families, especially during the ploughing and harvesting seasons. This form of voluntary work is known as *letsema*. The South African government has presently adopted the word *letsema* to encourage its citizens in volunteerism.

Sotho villages were also organized into age-sets, or groups of men or women who were close in age. Each age-set had specific responsibilities; men organized for warfare and herding, depending on age-set, and women for crop cultivation and religious responsibilities. An entire age-set generally graduated from one task to the next, and the village often celebrated this change with a series of rituals and, in some cases, an initiation ceremony. In the past initiations into adulthood were elaborate ceremonies lasting a few months, in which girls and boys were taken separately to the bush in the winter. The boys were circumcised. Increasingly, funerals have become the most elaborate life-cycle rituals.

Tswana groups are noted for their capacity to absorb foreign peoples, to turn strangers into 'their' people, and to do so without compromising the integrity of their own institutions. Socioeconomic mechanisms such as *mafisa* (which provided for the lending of cattle) and the ward system of tribal administration facilitated the integration of foreigners. Not all peoples were welcomed into the Tswana fold; some remained foreigners, and some became subjects. The latter category includes peoples of the desert (Bakgalagadi and Bushmen) who are accorded a servile status termed 'Batlhanka' or 'Boiata'.

Sotho descent rules were important, even though descent groups did not form discrete local groups. Clans were often totemic, or bound to specific natural objects or animal species by mystical relationships, sometimes involving taboos and prohibitions. Major Sotho clans included the Lion (Taung), Fish (Tlhaping), Elephant (Tloung), and Crocodile (Kwean) clans.

Nguni and Sotho people's marriage rules differed markedly. Sotho patrilineages were usually endogamous - i.e. the preferred marriage partner would be a person related through patrilineal descent ties. Nguni patrilineages, in contrast, were exogamous 'i.e. marriage within the descent group was generally forbidden.

Although the Tswana received Christian missionaries in the early nineteenth century and most belong to a church today, pre-colonial beliefs retain strength among many Tswana. Missionaries brought literacy, schools, and Western values, all of which facilitated the transition to migrant wage labor. In pre-colonial times Tswana believed in a Supreme Being, *Modimo*, a creator and director, but nonetheless distant and remote. More immediate and having a greater influence in daily affairs were the ancestors, *Badimo*. Most Tswana today belong to African Independent churches that incorporate Christian and non-Christian practices, beliefs, and symbols. The Tswana seek medical help from a number of sources, including clinics and hospitals, traditional practitioners, and Christian healers. For example, they still believe in consulting the traditional healer *ngak*, who is supposed to have powers to intercede on their behalf with the ancestors.

There are a few specialized Tswana arts; wood carving and basket weaving and beadwork is practiced by some and houses are often beautifully designed and painted. Song (*pina*) and dance (*pino*) are highly developed forms of artistic expression. Choirs perform and compete with each other on official and ritual occasions. They compose lyrics that offer narratives and critiques of the past and present.

The Tswana language is closely related to Sotho, and the two are mutually intelligible in most areas. Tswana is sometimes referred to as Beetjuans, Chuana (hence Bechuanaland), Coana, Cuana, or Sechuana. It is spoken across South Africa and is one of the 11 official languages recognized by the South African Constitution, it is also the national and majority language of Botswana. In 2006 it was determined that over 3 million South Africans speak Setswana as a home language.

Tswana was the one of the first written Sotho languages. The earliest example being Heinrich Lictenstein's 1806 text called *Upon the*

Language of the Beetjuana. Followed by John Cambell's *Bootchuana words* (1815) and Burchell's *Botswana in 1824*.

Dr Robert Moffat from the London Missionary Society went to Botsawana in 1818 and built the first school in the area. In 1825, he realised that he needed to use and write Setswana in his teachings. He therefore began translating the bible into Tswana; he completed *the New Testament* in 1840 and *the Old Testament* in 1857.

The first Motswana (singular) to contribute towards the writing of Setswana was Sol D. T. Plaatje, who assisted Professor Jones with the book on *The Tones of Sechuana Nouns* in 1929.

Origins:

The first pottery in South Africa associated with the Sotho is called *Icon* and dates to between 1300 and 1500. As with the Nguni, anthropological and linguistic data suggest an East African origin for Sotho-Tswana speakers, in this case in what is now Tanzania. By 1500 the Sotho groups had expanded to the south and west and separated into the three distinct clusters; the South Sotho (later became the Basuto and Sotho), the West Sotho (later the Tswana), and the North Sotho (later the Pedi). It is important to note however that all three clusters share very similar dialects, beliefs and society structures and the main distinctions between the three groups were only established as a result of the early 19th century *difiqane* period.

Most Sotho people were herders of cattle, goats, and sheep, and cultivators of grains and tobacco. In addition, the Sotho people were skilled craftsmen, renowned for their metalworking, leatherworking, and wood and ivory carving. In fact, most archaeologists presume the Sotho were the main body of early stone builders in this part of the country, because Iron Age sites studied by them resemble the areas reported by early eyewitnesses very closely.

In the 16th century, the Tswana settled in what was known as the Western Transvaal. They were divided into two main groups: the Tlhaping and Rolong under Chief Morolong (*the metal worker*) and the the Bafokeng (*people of the dew*). Oral traditions celebrate Morolong as *'the forger' who 'danced to iron'.*

In Botswana, the Tswana States started growing when the Kwena and Hurutshe migrants founded the Ngwaketse chiefdom among Khalagari-Rolong in south-eastern Botswana by 1700. They engaged in hunting, cattle raising, and copper production.

A period of warfare, political disruption, and migration commonly termed the *difiqane* (Zulu: *mfecane*) characterized the first quarter of the nineteenth century. The difiqane engendered a period of chaos, during which the Tswana experienced varying degrees of suffering, impoverishment, political disintegration, death, and forced movement. At the same time, however, some groups, particularly the western Tswana chiefdoms, eventually prospered and strengthened to the extent that they incorporated refugees and livestock.

European traders and missionaries (of the British nonconformist sects) began to arrive in the Tswana region in the first two decades of the nineteenth century. Trade (ivory, furs, and feathers being the most valued items) escalated after this period, and control over this trade dramatically empowered some Tswana chiefs, who were able to consolidate their control over extensive areas. By the mid-nineteenth century, Afrikaners, newly settled in the Transvaal, posed a threat to Tswana; Tswana chiefdoms acquired firearms to protect themselves, and many Tswana moved westward, into the area that is now Botswana. Christian missions were established throughout the region in the nineteenth century.

The discovery of diamonds and gold in the 1860s and 1870s in southern Africa led to the industrialization of South Africa and the introduction of the migrant-labor system, which continues to draw thousands of Tswana men to the mines (although recruitment from Botswana has been restricted since 1979). In 1885 the Bechuanaland

Protectorate was established in the north of the region, and, in the south, British Bechuanaland (now Republic of Botswana) was established as a Crown colony.

By the late nineteenth century, Afrikaner and British officials had seized almost all Tswana territory, dividing it among the Cape Colony, Afrikaner republics, and British territories. In 1910, when the Cape, Transvaal and British Bechuanaland were incorporated into the Union of South Africa, the Tswana chiefs lost most of their remaining power, and the Tswana people were forced to pay taxes to the British Crown. They gradually turned to migrant labor, especially in the mines, for their livelihood.

The dawn of apartheid in the 1940s marked more changes for all Black South Africans. In 1953 the South African Government introduced homelands; the Tswana in South Africa were declared citizens of Bophutaswana homeland, under the leadership of Chief Lucas Mangope. In 1977 Bophutatswana was granted nominal independence by South Africa, but no other nation recognized it. The homeland consisted primarily of seven disconnected enclaves near, or adjacent to, the border between South Africa and Botswana. Efforts to consolidate the territory and its population continued throughout the 1980s, as successive small land areas outside Bophuthatswana were incorporated into the homeland. Its population of about 1.8 million in the late 1980s was estimated to be 70 percent Tswana peoples; the remainder were other Sotho peoples, as well as Xhosa, Zulu, and Shangaan. Another 1.5 million Tswana lived elsewhere in South Africa.

Bophuthatswana's residents were overwhelmingly poor, despite the area's rich mineral wealth. Wages in the homeland's industrial sector were lower than those in South Africa, and most workers traveled to jobs outside the homeland each day. The poverty of homeland residents was especially evident in comparison with the world's wealthy tourists who visited Sun City, a gambling resort in Bophuthatswana.

The non-Tswana portion of the homeland population was denied the right to vote in local elections in 1987, and violence ensued. Further unrest erupted in early 1988, when members of the Botswana Defence Force tried to oust the unpopular homeland president, Lucas Mangope. Escalating violence after that led to the imposition of states of emergency and government crackdowns against ANC supporters in Bophuthatswana, who were often involved in anti-Mangope demonstrations. Mangope was ousted just before the April 1994 elections, and the homeland was officially dismantled after the elections.

Venda

As with most of the other peoples of South Africa the Venda (VhaVenda) came from the Great Lakes of Central Africa. They first settled down in the Soutpansberg Mountains. Here they built their first capital, D'zata, the ruins of which can still be seen today. Venda culture has an interesting mix of other cultures - it appears to have incorporated a variety of East African, Central African, Nguni, and Sotho characteristics. For example, the Venda forbid the consumption of pork, a prohibition that is common along the East African coast.

They also practice male circumcision, which is common among many Sotho, but not among most Nguni peoples.The Venda language, TshiVenda or LuVenda, emerged as a distinct dialect in the 16th Century. In the 20th Century, the TshiVenda vocabulary was similar to SeSotho, but the grammar shares similarities with Shona dialects, which are spoken in Zimbabwe. Today about 875 000 people in South Africa speak Tshivenda. The history of the Venda starts from the Mapungubwe Kingdom (9th Century). According to historical studies King Shiriyadenga was the first king of Venda and Mapungubwe. Shiriyadenga was succeeded by his children.

Historical Background:

From 800AD, the Mapungubwe Kingdom emerged, stretching from the Soutpansberg in the south, across the Limpopo River to the Matopos in the north. The Mapungubwe Kingdom declined from 1240, and the centre of power and trade moved north to the Great Zimbabwe Kingdom. A shifting of focus to Zimbabwe's Khami and Rozwi empires followed, but the culture did not come to a standstill. South of the Limpopo Shona-Venda and Venda pottery styles developed in the 14th and 15th Centuries. There are no stonewalled ruins comparable in size to Great Zimbabwe in the northeastern part of Northern Province, but those in the mountains show a link.Accompanying the development of these centres, from about 1400, waves of Shona-speaking migrants from modern Zimbabwe (known by the Venda as Thavatsindi) settled across the Lowveld. The Venda are generally regarded as one of the last black groups to have entered the area south of the Limpopo River.

Their history is closely related to the history of their successive captains' houses, especially those who were descended from their legendary ancestor, Thoho-ya-Ndou (Head of the Elephant).Thoho-ya-Ndou's kraal (home) was called D'zata and the remains of this have been declared a National Monument. D'zata had great significance for the Venda because they buried their chiefs facing it. When Thoho-ya-

Ndou died, divisions arose between the different captains' houses as a result of disputes regarding the question of who was to succeed him.

In Venda tradition, succession to the throne is a complex matter and their history has been characterised by many disputes over occupancy of the throne. Today there are 26 captains' houses that trace their origins to the great man while a few others trace their ancestry to tribes that were later incorporated with the Venda. However, the true Venda can be divided into 2 groups, namely a western group, primarily of Singo origin and descended from the followers of leaders such as Mphephu, Senthumule and Kutama; and an eastern group who regarded themselves as descendants of Lwamonde, Rambuda, Tshivashe and Mphapuli.

It was believed that the Singo king could protect his people from attack by their enemies by beating a special drum called the Ngoma Lungundo, ('drum of the dead'). According to legend, the sound of the drum would strike terror in the hearts of the enemy and they would flee. Some Venda say that this king disappeared from his kraal one night with this special drum and neither were ever seen again. It is believed that at Mashovhela"place where the drums can be heard", rock pool on the Morning Sun Nature Reserve, you can still hear the his drum in the echoes of the cliffs and is considered the second most sacred site in Venda culture. One of the most interesting and distinct groups of people who later joined the Venda are the African Semites, the Lemba.

They are believed to be the descendants of Semitic (Arab) traders who entered Africa around 696AD. The Lemba believe themselves to be Black Jews, descendants of the lost tribe of Israel. They keep to themselves, only marry within their own group and sometimes refer to themselves as Vhalungu, which means 'non-Negroid' or 'respected foreigner'. The beads they brought with them from these far-off countries are still treasured to this day and are used in divination and other magical ceremonies. The Lemba were very good traders and artisans. They were also famous, for their metalwork and pottery.

The first contact between the Venda and the whites occurred when the Voortrekker leader, Louis Trichardt came to the area in 1836.In 1848, the whites established a settlement named Schoemansdal. However, Makhado, the Venda captain at the time, harassed the white settlers to such an extent that they abandoned the town in 1867. This harassment was continued by Makhado's son, Mphephu and eventually led to the Mphephu War when he was defeated and had to flee to Zimbabwe. During the Apartheid period, a homeland was set aside for the Venda people. It covered 6 500 square kilometres and the capital city was called Thohoyandou in honour of the great Venda chief of the same name. It became independent in 1979. Today, the area is once again part of South Africa; located in the Limpopo Province.

Social & Cultural Life

Trade, warfare and intermarriage with Tsonga, Lobedu, Zulu, Swazi and other people, have also left their imprints on Venda culture. The Venda were a protective people, many of whom still practiced polygamy and worshipped their families' ancestors. Members of the different clans could, and did, live in any of the tribal territories, because the tribe was purely a political and territorial unit, consisting of people who chose to owe allegiance to a particular dynasty. It was quite common to find a ruler attracting members of his own clan after his accession. There was no paramount chief each tribe was ruled by an independent chief, who had under him headmen, responsible for the government of districts within the tribal territory.

Most of the chiefs belonged to lineages of the same clan, which crossed the Limpopo River and controlled those whom they found living in the Zoutpansberg in the latter half of the 18th century. Thus there was an important social division in Venda society between commoners (vhasiwana) and the children of chiefs and their descendants (vhakololo). In the Sibasa district (located in Northern Province) there were 12 Venda chiefs some were the descendants of brothers, who were the sons of a ruling chief but broke away and established independent chiefdoms elsewhere. There were a number of differences in the customs of the various clans, especially in religious ritual, but there were no distinct differences between the tribes.

Venda Belief System

The Venda culture is built on a vibrant mythical belief system, which is reflected in their artistic style. Water is an important theme to the Venda and there are many sacred sites within their region where the Venda conjure up their ancestral spirits. They believe zwidutwane, (water spirits), live at the bottom of waterfalls. These beings are only half-visible; they only have one eye, one leg, and one arm. One half can be seen in this world and the other half in the spirit world. The Venda would take offerings of food to them because the zwidutwane cannot grow things underwater.One of the most sacred sites of the Venda is Lake Fundudzi. Suspicion surrounds the lake, which is fed by the Mutale River yet does not appear to have an outlet. It is also said that you can sometimes hear the Tshikona song although no one appears to be there. The Venda people have a very special relationship with Crocodiles. The area where they live is filled with these dangerous reptiles. The Venda believe that the brain of the Crocodile is very poisonous, therefore they are given right of way by the Venda who do not even hunt them for food.

Venda Rituals

Initiation:

The Domba is a pre-marital initiation, the last one in the life of a Venda girl or boy. The chief or sovereign will 'call' a domba and preparations are made by the families for their girls to be ready and to prepare what's necessary to attend the ceremony (entry fees for the ruler, clothes and bangles). Historically girls used to stay with the chief for the whole duration (3 months to 3 years) of the initiation; nowadays because of schooling, girls only spend weekends at the ruler's kraal. This rite of passage was attended by both girls and boys after each individual had previously attended other separated initiations dedicated to one's gender; Vusha and Tshikanda for girls and Murundu for boys (the circumcision done during this rite has been introduced by North Sotho). Since the missionaries decided that mixing males and females in the same ceremony was immoral. Only girls attend the Domba which has two main functions teaching girls how to prepare themselves to become wives (birth planning, giving birth and child care, how to treat a husband, and nowadays the teaching of AIDS risks); and bringing fertility to the new generation of the tribe.

Music and Dance

Various rituals are particular to the Venda and certain aspects are kept secret and not discussed with westerners, however, it is known that the python dance, conducted at the female coming of age ceremony (iconic to the Limpopo region) is usually where the chief chooses a wife. Girls and boys dance fluidly, like a snake, to the beat of a drum, while forming a chain by holding the forearm of the person in front. Once a wife has been chosen a set of courtship and grooming rituals take place over a number of days.

The tshikona is traditionally a male dance in which each player has a pipe made out of a special indigenous type of bamboo growing only in few places around Sibasa and Thohoyandou (which no longer exists). Each player has one note to play, which has to be played in turn, in such a way as to build a melody. The tshikona is a royal dance, each sovereign or chief has his own tshikona band. Tshikona is played at various occasions for funerals, wedding or religious ceremonies, this can be considered as the Venda 'national music / dance', which is particular to Venda in South Africa.

The tshigombela is a female dance usually performed by married women, this is a festive dance sometimes played at the same time as tshikona. Tshifhasi is similar to tshigombela but performed by young unmarried girls (khomba). The Mbila is played in the north of South Africa and more particularly by the Venda. It can be described as a keyboard made out of a piece of wood, which is the resonator, and with metal blades (made out of huge nails hammered flat) which are the keys.

While the Mbila is still widely played in Zimbabwe, in South Africa it is only played by a few old people, who sadly notice that most youngsters are disinterested in their own culture and let it die. The playing of the Mbila is one of the most endangered Venda traditions. The Venda style of playing Mbila is quite different from that of Zimbabwe or Mozambique.

Drums are central in Venda culture and there are legends and symbols linked to them. Most sets of drums are kept in the homes of chiefs and headmen, and comprise one ngoma, one thungwa, and 2 or 3 murumba.

Drum sets without the Ngoma may be found in the homes of certain members of the tribe, such as the doctors who run girls' 'circumcision' schools. Drums are often given personal names. Drums are always played by women and girls, except in possession dances, when men may play them.

Venda Today

Under the apartheid system the land of the Venda people was designated a homeland so they were fairly unaffected by the political and social changes that had such a massive affect on the rest of the country.

The 1 000 000 strong Venda population was left alone to live the way they had for hundreds of years in their lush, mountainous and remote region, which is why their culture, language, arts and crafts have survived so strongly. Today, many Venda people live in Thohoyandou in the Limpopo. It is situated not far from the border of Zimbabwe

Xhosa

Xhosa

The four major ethnic divisions among Black South Africans are the Nguni, Sotho, Shangaan-Tsonga and Venda. The Nguni represent nearly two thirds of South Africa's Black population and can be divided into four distinct groups; the Northern and Central Nguni (the Zulu-speaking peoples), the Southern Nguni (the Xhosa-speaking peoples), the Swazi people from Swaziland and adjacent areas and the Ndebele people of the Northern Province and Mpumalanga. Archaeological evidence shows that the Bantu-speaking groups that were the ancestors of the Nguni migrated down from East Africa as early as the eleventh century.

Language, culture and beliefs:

The Xhosa are the second largest cultural group in South Africa, after the Zulu-speaking nation. The Xhosa language (Isixhosa), of which there are variations, is part of the Nguni language group. Xhosa is one of the 11 official languages recognized by the South African Constitution, and in 2006 it was determined that just over 7 million South Africans speak Xhosa as a home language. It is a tonal language, governed by the noun - which dominates the sentence.

Missionaries introduced the Xhosa to Western choral singing. Among the most successful of the Xhosa hymns is the South African national anthem, *Nkosi Sikele' iAfrika* (God Bless Africa). It was written by a school teacher named Enoch Sontonga in 1897. Xhosa written literature was established in the nineteenth century with the publication of the first Xhosa newspapers, novels, and plays. Early writers included Tiyo Soga, I. Bud-Mbelle, and John Tengo Jabavu.

Stories and legends provide accounts of Xhosa ancestral heroes. According to one oral tradition, the first person on Earth was a great leader called Xhosa. Another tradition stresses the essential unity of the Xhosa-speaking people by proclaiming that all the Xhosa subgroups are descendants of one ancestor, Tshawe. Historians have suggested that Xhosa and Tshawe were probably the first Xhosa kings or paramount (supreme) chiefs.

The Supreme Being among the Xhosa is called *uThixo or uQamata*. As in the religions of many other Bantu peoples, God is only rarely involved in everyday life. God may be approached through ancestral intermediaries who are honoured through ritual sacrifices. Ancestors commonly make their wishes known to the living in dreams. Xhosa religious practice is distinguished by elaborate and lengthy rituals, initiations, and feasts. Modern rituals typically pertain to matters of illness and psychological well-being.

The Xhosa people have various rites of passage traditions. The first of these occurs after giving birth; a mother is expected to remain secluded in her house for at least ten days. In Xhosa tradition, the afterbirth and umbilical cord were buried or burned to protect the baby from sorcery. At the end of the period of seclusion, a goat was sacrificed. Those who no longer practice the traditional rituals may still invite friends and relatives to a special dinner to mark the end of the mother's seclusion.

Male and female initiation in the form of circumcision is practiced among most Xhosa groups. The Male *abakweta* (initiates-in-training) live in special huts isolated from villages or towns for several weeks. Like soldiers inducted into the army, they have their heads shaved. They wear a loincloth and a blanket for warmth, and white clay is smeared on their bodies from head to toe. They are expected to observe numerous taboos (prohibitions) and to act deferentially to their adult male leaders. Different stages in the initiation process were marked by the sacrifice of a goat.

The ritual of female circumcision is considerably shorter. The intonjane (girl to be initiated) is secluded for about a week. During this period, there are dances, and ritual sacrifices of animals. The initiate must hide herself from view and observe food restrictions. There is no actual surgical operation.

Origins:

Although they speak a common language, Xhosa people belong to many loosely organized, but distinct chiefdoms that have their origins in their Nguni ancestors. It is important to question how and why the

Nguni speakers were separated into the sub-group known today. The majority of central northern Nguni people became part of the Zulu kingdom, whose language and traditions are very similar to the Xhosa nations - the main difference is that the latter abolished circumcision.

In order to understand the origins of the Xhosa people we must examine the developments of the southern Nguni, who intermarried with Khoikhoi and retained circumcision. For unknown reasons, certain southern Nguni groups began to expand their power some time before 1600. Tshawe founded the Xhosa kingdom by defeating the Cirha and Jwarha groups. His descendants expanded the kingdom by settling in new territory and bringing people living there under the control of the amaTshawe. Generally, the group would take on the name of the chief under whom they had united. There are therefore distinct varieties of the Xhosa language, the most distinct being *isiMpondo (isiNdrondroza)*. Other dialects include: Thembu, Bomvana, Mpondimise, Rharhabe, Gcaleka, Xesibe, Bhaca, Cele, Hlubi, Ntlangwini, Ngqika, Mfengu (also names of different groups or clans).

Unlike the Zulu and the Ndebele in the north, the position of the king as head of a lineage did not make him an absolute king. The junior chiefs of the various chiefdoms acknowledged and deferred to the paramount chief in matters of ceremony, law, and tribute, but he was not allowed to interfere in their domestic affairs. There was great rivalry among them, and few of these leaders could answer for the actions of even their own councillors. As they could not centralise their power, chiefs were constantly preoccupied with strategies to maintain the loyalties of their followers.

The Cape Nguni of long ago were cattle farmers. They took great care of their cattle because they were a symbol of wealth, status, and respect. Cattle were used to determine the price of a bride, or lobola, and they were the most acceptable offerings to the ancestral spirits. They also kept dogs, goats and later, horses, sheep, pigs and poultry. Their chief crops were millet, maize, kidney beans, pumpkins, and watermelons. By the eighteenth century they were also growing tobacco and hemp.

At this stage isiXhosa was not a written language but there was a rich store of music and oral poetry. Xhosa tradition is rich in creative verbal expression. *Intsomi* (folktales), proverbs, and *isibongo* (praise poems) are told in dramatic and creative ways. Folktales relate the adventures of both animal protagonists and human characters. Praise poems traditionally relate the heroic adventures of ancestors or political leaders.

As the Xhosa slowly moved westwards in groups, they destroyed or incorporated the Khoikhoi chiefdoms and San groups, and their language became influenced by Khoi and San words, which contain distinctive 'clicks'.

Europeans who came to stay in South Africa first settled in and around Cape Town. As the years passed, they sought to expand their territory. This expansion was first at the expense of the Khoi and San, but later Xhosa land was taken as well. The Xhosa encountered eastward-moving White pioneers or 'Trek Boers' in the region of the Fish River. The ensuing struggle was not so much a contest between Black and White races as a struggle for water, grazing and living space between two groups of farmers.

Nine Frontier Wars followed between the Xhosa and European settlers, and these wars dominated 19th century South African History. The first frontier war broke out in 1780 and marked the beginning of the Xhosa struggle to preserve their traditional customs and way of life. It was a struggle that was to increase in intensity when the British arrived on the scene.

The Xhosa fought for one hundred years to preserve their independence, heritage and land, and today this area is still referred to by many as Frontier Country.

During the Frontier Wars, hostile chiefs forced the earliest missionaries to abandon their attempts to 'evangelise' them. This situation changed after 1820, when John Brownlee founded a mission on the Tyhume River near Alice, and William Shaw established a chain of Methodist stations throughout the Transkei.

Other denominations followed suit. Education and medical work were to become major contributions of the missions, and today Xhosa cultural traditionalists are likely to belong to independent denominations that combine Christianity with traditional beliefs and practices. In addition to land lost to white annexation, legislation reduced Xhosa political autonomy. Over time, Xhosa people became increasingly impoverished, and had no option but to become migrant labourers. In the late 1990s, Xhosa labourers made up a large percentage of the workers in South Africa's gold mines.

The dawn of apartheid in the 1940s marked more changes for all Black South Africans. In 1953 the South African Government introduced homelands or Bantustans, and two regions 'Transkei and Ciskei' were set aside for Xhosa people. These regions were proclaimed independent countries by the apartheid government. Therefore many Xhosa were denied South African citizenship, and thousands were forcibly relocated to remote areas in Transkei and Ciskei.

The homelands were abolished with the change to democracy in 1994 and South Africa's first democratically elected president was African National Congress (ANC) leader, Nelson Mandela, who is a Xhosa-speaking member of the Thembu people.

Social and Cultural Life

The earliest Xhosa homesteads consisted of a circular frame of poles and young trees bent and bound together in the shape of a beehive and covered from top to bottom with grass. During the early 1820s, traditional construction methods changed and huts were built with circular walls of coated stakes interwoven with branches and having thatched conical roofs. The individual huts that formed a homestead were usually built in a semi-circle around a circular cattle enclosure. Under the floor of the cattle enclosure, the Xhosas stored maize in bottle-shaped pits. The pits were well plastered and the openings closed with stones to prevent the maize from being spoilt.

Although the maize gave off a bad smell and tasted sour, it was a good stand-by when food was in short supply. The cooking areas, on the outside of the houses, were screened off and consisted of a clay oven for baking maize bread and some bins for storing corncobs. The area between the door of the main house and the opening of the cattle enclosure was always neatly swept and was called the courtyard. Here the chief would hold court cases. Each homestead was an independent unit with its own livestock and lands. The Xhosa people enjoyed physical closeness and mothers carried their babies on their backs, close to their bodies, from the moment the baby was born. The Xhosa home was usually quite small and the family members lived in close proximity to each other. Friends were automatically included as part of the community and the family.

Sharing Nature

The Xhosa had a deep sense of community and would extend a helping hand to anyone in need. The way in which food was cooked, on an open fire in a cast-iron pot, where everyone could come and help himself/herself, was indicative of their sharing nature. Maize was the staple food. The Xhosa were also very fond of their beer, made from sorghum and maize.

Initiation

Before a Xhosa male was recognised as an adult with the right to marry, he first had to go through the initiation process and be circumcised. Until such time, he was regarded as a boy and irresponsibility on his part was expected and condoned. Only boys who were considered ready were allowed to undergo initiation. The ceremony usually took place when the corn ripened, during the month of May. On the agreed day, the married women emerged at dawn and started building a grass hut for the boys. The boys waited in a secluded spot for arrival of the surgeon who would perform the circumcision.

The boys were not allowed to utter any sound during the procedure. After the wounds had healed, the boys undertook excursions into the bush where they hunted.A small boy from their village accompanied each. Sometimes they would be joined by one of the senior and respected men from the village, who would teach them how to behave like responsible adults. This teaching included the rules of etiquette, the laws of respect and how to honour the ancestral spirits.

At intervals, the young men staged dances, called Amakwetha, showing off their dancingskills while they proceeded from home to home. They disguised themselves in headdresses, wore heavy skirts of palm leaves and painted their bodies with white clay.At the end of the isolation period, the initiates were marched down to the river to wash themselves. Upon returning, their guide then placed a piece of fat on their heads and smeared it straight down their bodies and across their shoulders, in the form of a cross. After this ritual, the boys wrapped themselves in brand new blankets and turned away from the hut, covering their faces. All their possessions were thrown into the hut and then set alight, to prevent witches from taking possession of these things.

They were also forbidden to look back. The amakrwala, as these boy-men were called, were then marched back to their parental homes where they were showered with gifts and a feast was prepared in their honour. After the feast was over, the young men went indoors where girls of their own age helped them to smear themselves from top to bottom with a mixture of oil and red ochre. Every day, for the following year, the boy had to refresh his red ochre. He also had to walk slowly to demonstrate his humility and to signify that he was still a "small', unimportant man. While the males of the tribe underwent their initiation, girls of the same age had their heads shaven and were dressed in a specific manner for a few weeks. When the male initiates emerged from their isolation, the girls were recognised as being of marriageable age.

Courtship and marriage

The traditional Xhosa was allowed to have more than one wife. Xhosa tradition made provision for a certain degree of contact and courtship between sweethearts but proper form demanded that girls remain virgins until they married. If a girl was not a virgin, her father would automatically receive less lobola (bride price) for her. Traditionally, the groom-to-be would abduct the bride, with the approval of her family, and then marry her. Today, marriage only involves the exchange of valuables. The bride's father pays a dowry to his daughter's future in-laws and the bridegroom has to pay lobola for the bride.

Personal Adornment

For generations the Xhosa people have been referred to as the Red Blanket People. This was because of their custom of wearing red blankets dyed with red ochre, the intensity of the colour varying from tribe to tribe. The different ways in which clothes and other accessories were worn signalled the status of the wearer. Unmarried women wore wraps tied around their shoulders, leaving their breasts exposed. Engaged women reddened their plaited hair, letting it screen their eyes, as a sign of respect for their fiancés.Xhosa females always wore some form of headdress, as a sign of respect to the head of the family, either their father or husband.

Older Xhosa women were allowed to wear more elaborate headpieces because of their seniority. The various tribes had their own different forms of traditional dress and the colour of their garments and the adornments they wore denoted their tribal origins. The Xhosa tribe itself consisted of two major clans that could be distinguished from one another bytheir different styles of dress. The Gcaleka women, for example, encased their arms and legs in beads and brass bangles and some also wore neck beads. Men often wore goatskin bags in which to carry essentials such as homegrown tobacco and a knife. Making the bag required great skill and patience as it had to be made from skin that had been removed in one piece, cured without removing the hair, and turned inside out.

Art and Crafts

Other than the beadwork used for their traditional dress and their pipes made of clay, the Xhosa people were not really known for any other arts and crafts. The girls of the family usually produced the beadwork, helping their mothers to make articles for themselves, their fathers, brothers and boyfriends. From time to time they were permitted to borrow these pieces and to wear them themselves.

Music and Dance

Dancing formed an integral part of the Xhosa culture and was part and parcel of most of the rituals. Dancing was, for example, used in the "fattening of the maize" ceremony and as part of the ritual to ensure the fertility of a friend before she married or to restore her fertility if she had trouble bearing children after the marriage. Men and women and boys and girls did not dance in pairs. They lined up opposite each other.

Belief System

The Xhosa people are traditionally ancestor worshippers but also believe in a creator who cares for them in the greater things in life and who protects them in extreme danger. The ancestral fathers, on the other hand, watch over the everyday lives of their descendants, their crops and their cattle. Among the Xhosa, old people are revered as spirits, and sacrificial offerings may actually be made to them while they are still alive. The ancestral fathers also speak to their families in dreams. However, because not everyone is capable of interpreting these dreams, witchdoctors are called in to act as mediums.

They are easily recognisable by their exotic regalia and they often wear white - a symbol of purity. Death and burial are associated with many complex beliefs and rituals.The men of the clan always lead the funeral procession and the women follow behind. In the case of the death of the head of the family, cattle will be sacrificed and strict procedures followed, as he goes to join his ancestors and prepares himself to watch after the interests of the family that is left behind. Today, many of the Xhosa-speaking people of South Africa are Christians, as a result of their early contact with European missionaries. However, their religion has become a unique blend of Christianity and traditional African beliefs.

Zulu

The four major ethnic divisions among Black South Africans are the Nguni, Sotho, Shangaan-Tsonga and Venda. The Nguni represent nearly two thirds of South Africa's Black population and can be divided into four distinct groups; the Northern and Central Nguni (the Zulu-speaking peoples), the Southern Nguni (the Xhosa-speaking peoples), the Swazi people from Swaziland and adjacent areas, and the Ndebele people of the Northern Province and Mpumalanga. Archaeological evidence shows that the Bantu-speaking groups, that were the ancestors of the Nguni, migrated down from East Africa as early as the eleventh century.

Language, culture and beliefs:

The Zulu language, of which there are variations, is part of the Nguni language group. The word Zulu means "Sky" and according to oral history, Zulu was the name of the ancestor who founded the Zulu royal line in about 1670. Today it is estimated that there are more than 45 million South Africans, and the Zulu people make up about approximately 22% of this number. The largest urban concentration of

Zulu people is in the Gauteng Province, and in the corridor of Pietermaritzburg and Durban. The largest rural concentration of Zulu people is in Kwa-Zulu Natal.

IsiZulu is South Africa's most widely spoken official language. It is a tonal language understood by people from the Cape to Zimbabwe and is characterized by many "clicks". In 2006 it was determined that approximately 9 million South Africans speak Xhosa as a home language.

The following overview of the language was written by B.P. Mngadi for UNESCO's World Languages Report (2000):

"The writing of Zulu was started by missionaries in the then Natal. The names J W Colenso, S B Stone, H Callaway and Lewis Grant are among the prominent. They taught the first people with whom they made contact, spreading the word of God, basic writing skills in Zulu. Magema Fuze, Ndiyane and William were among the very first who were taught communicative English and basic writing skills at about 1830-1841. The first Zulu Christian booklet was produced by Newton Adams, George Newton and Aldin Grout (1837-8) titled "Incwadi Yokuqala Yabafundayo" which dealt with spelling of Zulu words and the history of the Old Testament. Between 1845 and 1883, the first translated version of the Bible was produced in very old Zulu

orthography. In 1859 the first Zulu Grammar Book by L. Grout was produced".

Its oral tradition is very rich but its modern literature is still developing. J.L Dube was the first Zulu writer (1832) though his first publication was a Zulu story written in English titled *"A Talk on my Native Land"*. In 1903 he concentrated in editing the newspaper *"Ilanga LaseNatali"*. His first Zulu novel *"Insila kaShaka"* was published in 1930. We see a steady growth of publications especially novels from 1930 onwards.

The clear-cut distinction made today between the Xhosa and the Zulu has no basis in culture or history, but arises out of the colonial distinction between the Cape and Natal colonies. Both speak very similar languages and share similar customs, but the historical experiences at the northern end of the Nguni culture area differed considerably from the historical experiences at the southern end. The majority of northerners became part of the Zulu kingdom, which abolished circumcision. The majority of southerners never became part of any strongly centralised kingdom, intermarried with Khoikhoi and retained circumcision.

Many Zulu people converted to Christianity under colonialism. However, although there are many Christian converts, ancestral beliefs have not disappeared. Instead, there has been a mixture of traditional beliefs and Christianity. Ancestral spirits are important in Zulu religious life ,and offerings and sacrifices are made to the ancestors for protection, good health, and happiness. Ancestral spirits come back to the world in the form of dreams, illnesses, and sometimes snakes. The Zulu also believe in the use of magic. Ill fortune such as bad luck and illness is considered to be sent by an angry spirit. When this happens, the help of a traditional healer is sought, and he or she will communicate with the ancestors, or use natural herbs and prayers, to get rid of the problem.

Late nineteenth century postcard of Zulu Warriors
(note the Europeans in the background)

The Zulu are fond of singing as well as dancing. These activities promote unity at all the transitional ceremonies such as births, weddings, and funerals. All the dances are accompanied by drums and the men dress as warriors (see image).

Zulu folklore is transmitted through storytelling, praise-poems, and proverbs. These explain Zulu history and teach moral lessons. Praise-poems (poems recited about the kings and the high achievers in life) are becoming part of popular culture. The Zulu, especially those from rural areas, are known for their weaving, craft-making, pottery, and beadwork.

The Zulu term for "family" (umndeni) includes all the people staying in a homestead who are related to each other, either by blood, marriage, or adoption. Drinking and eating from the same plate was and still is a sign of friendship. It is customary for children to eat from the same dish, usually a big basin. This derives from a "share what you have" belief which is part of ubuntu (humane) philosophy.

Origins:

Long ago, before the Zulu were forged as a nation, they lived as isolated family groups and partly nomadic northern Nguni groups. These groups moved about within their loosely defined territories in search of game and good grazing for their cattle. As they accumulated livestock, and supporters family leaders divided and dispersed in different directions, while still retaining family networks.

The Zulu homestead (imizi) consisted of an extended family and others attached to the household through social obligations. This social unit was largely self-sufficient, with responsibilities divided according to gender. Men were generally responsible for defending the homestead, caring for cattle, manufacturing and maintaining weapons and farm implements, and building dwellings. Women had domestic responsibilities and raised crops, usually grains, on land near the household.

By the late eighteenth century, a process of political consolidation among the groups was beginning to take place. A number of powerful chiefdoms began to emerge and a transformation from pastoral society to a more organised statehood occurred. This enabled leaders to wield more authority over their own supporters, and to compel allegiance from conquered chiefdoms. Changes took place in the nature of political, social, and economic links between chiefs of these emerging power blocs and their subjects. Zulu chiefs demanded steadily increasing tribute or taxes from their subjects, acquired great wealth, commanded large armies, and, in many cases, subjugated neighbouring chiefdoms.

Military conquest allowed men to achieve status distinctions that had become increasingly important. This culminated early in the nineteenth century with the warrior-king Shaka conquering all the groups in Zululand and uniting them into a single powerful Zulu nation, that made its influence felt over southern and central Africa. Shaka ruled from 1816 to 1828, when he was assassinated by his brothers.

Shaka recruited young men from all over the kingdom and trained them in his own novel warrior tactics. His military campaign resulted in widespread violence and displacement, and after defeating competing armies and assimilating their people, Shaka established his Zulu nation. Within twelve years, he had forged one of the mightiest empires the African continent has ever known. The Zulu empire weakened after Shaka's death in 1828.

One of the most significant events in Zulu history was the arrival of Europeans in Natal. By the late 1800s, British troops had invaded Zulu territory and divided Zulu land into different chiefdoms. The Zulu never regained their independence .

Natal received "Colonial government" in 1893, and the Zulu people were dissatisfied about being governed by the Colony. A plague of locusts devastated crops in Zululand and Natal in 1894 and 1895, and their cattle were dying of rinderpest, lung sickness and east coast fever. These natural disasters impoverished them and forced more men to seek employment as railway construction workers in northern Natal and on the mines in the Witwatersrand.

The last Zulu uprising, led by Chief Bambatha in 1906, was a response to harsh and unjust laws and unimaginable actions by the Natal Government. It was sparked off by the imposition of the 1905 poll tax of £1 per head, introduced to increase revenue and to force more Zulus to start working for wages. The uprising was ruthlessly suppressed.

The 1920s saw fundamental changes in the Zulu nation. Many were drawn towards the mines and fast-growing cities as wage earners, and were separated from the land and urbanised. Zulu men and women have made up a substantial portion of South Africa's urban work force throughout the 20th century, especially in the gold and copper mines of the Witwatersrand. Zulu workers organized some of the first black labour unions in the country. For example, the Zulu Washermen's Guild, Amawasha, was active in Natal and the Witwatersrand even before the Union of South Africa was formed in 1910. The Zululand Planters' Union organized agricultural workers in Natal in the early twentieth century.

The dawn of apartheid in the 1940s marked more changes for all Black South Africans, and in 1953 the South African Government introduced the "homelands". In the 1960s the Government's objective was to form a "tribal authority" and provide for the gradual development of self-governing Bantu national units. The first Territorial Authority for the Zulu people was established in 1970 and the Zulu homeland of KwaZulu was defined. On 30 March 1972 the first Legislative Assembly of KwaZulu was constituted by South African Parliamentary Proclamation.

Chief Mangosutho (Gatsha) Buthelezi, a cousin of the king, was elected as Chief Executive. The town of Nongoma was temporarily consolidated as the capital, pending completion of buildings at Ulundi. The 1970s also saw the revival of Inkatha, later the Inkatha Freedom Party (IFP), the ruling and sole party in the self-governing KwaZulu homeland. Led by Chief Minister Mangosutho Buthelezi, Inkatha worked within the NP governments system, but it opposed homeland independence, standing for non-racial democracy, federalism, and free enterprise.

Military prowess continued to be an important value in Zulu culture, and this emphasis fuelled some of the political violence of the 1990s. Buthelezi's nephew, Goodwill Zwelithini, was the Zulu monarch in the 1990s. Buthelezi and King Goodwill won the agreement of ANC negotiators just before the April 1994 elections that, with international mediation, the government would establish a special status for the Zulu Kingdom after the elections. Zulu leaders understood this special status to mean some degree of regional autonomy within the province of KwaZulu-Natal.

Buthelezi was appointed minister of home affairs in the first Government of National Unity in 1994. He led a walkout of Zulu delegates from the National Assembly in early 1995 and clashed repeatedly with newly elected President Nelson (Rolihlahla) Mandela. Buthelezi threatened to abandon the Government of National Unity entirely unless his Zulu constituency received greater recognition and autonomy from central government control

Biographies
Sara 'Saartjie' Baartman

Sara 'Saartjie' Baartman was born in 1789* at the Gamtoos river in what is now known as the Eastern Cape. She belonged to the cattle-herding Gonaquasub group of the Khoikhoi. Sara grew up on a colonial farm where her family most probably worked as servants. Her mother died when she was aged two and her father, who was a cattle driver, died when she reached adolescence. Sara married a Khoikhoi man who was a drummer and they had one child together who died shortly after birth.

Due to colonial expansion, the Dutch came into conflict with the Khoikhoi. As a result people were gradually absorbed into the labour system. When she was sixteen years old Sara's fiancé was murdered by Dutch colonists. Soon after, she was sold into slavery to a trader named Pieter Willem Cezar, who took her to Cape Town where she became a domestic servant to his brother. It was during this time that she was given the name 'Saartjie', a Dutch diminutive for Sara.

On 29 October 1810, Sara allegedly 'signed' a contract with an English ship surgeon named William Dunlop who was also a friend of Cezar and his brother Hendrik. Apparently, the terms of her 'contract' were that she would travel with Hendrik Cezar and Dunlop to England and Ireland to work as a domestic servant, and be exhibited for entertainment purposes. She was to receive a 'portion of earnings' from her exhibitions and be allowed to return to South Africa after five years. Two reasons make her 'signing' appear dubious. The first is that she was illiterate and came from a cultural tradition that did not write or keep records. Secondly, the Cezar families experienced financial woes and it is suspected that they used Sara to earn money.

Sara Baartman's large buttocks and unusual colouring made her the object of fascination by the colonial Europeans who presumed that they were racially superior. Dunlop wanted Sara to come to London and become an oddity for display. She was taken to London where she was displayed in a building in Piccadilly, a street that was full of various oddities like "the ne plus ultra of hideousness" and "the greatest deformity in the world". Englishmen and women paid to see Sara's half naked body displayed in a cage that was about a metre and half high. She became an attraction for people from various parts of Europe.

During her time with Dunlop and Hendrik Cezar, the campaign against slavery in Britain was in full swing and as a result, the treatment of Baartman was called into question. Her "employers" were brought to trial but faced no real consequences. They produced a document that had allegedly been signed by Sara Baartman and her own testimony which claimed that she was not being mistreated. Her 'contract' was, however, amended and she became entitled to 'better conditions', greater profit share and warm clothes.

After four years in London, in September 1814, she was transported from England to France, and upon arrival Hendrik Cezar sold her to Reaux, a man who showcased animals. He exhibited her around Paris and reaped financial benefits from the public's fascination with Sara's body. He began exhibiting her in a cage alongside a baby rhinoceros. Her "trainer" would order her to sit or stand in a similar way that circus animals are ordered. At times Baartman was displayed almost completely naked, wearing little more than a tan loincloth, and she was only allowed that due to her insistence that she cover what was culturally sacred. She was nicknamed "Hottentot Venus".

Her constant display attracted the attention of George Cuvier, a naturalist. He asked Reaux if he would allow Sara to be studied as a science specimen to which Reaux agreed. As from March 1815 Sara was studied by French anatomists, zoologists and physiologists. Cuvier concluded that she was a link between animals and humans. Thus, Sara was used to help emphasise the stereotype that Africans were oversexed and a lesser race.

Sara Baartman died in 1816 at the age of 26. It is unknown whether she died from alcoholism, smallpox or pneumonia. Cuvier obtained her remains from local police and dissected her body. He made a plaster cast of her body, pickled her brain and genitals and placed them into jars which were placed on display at the *Musée de l'Homme (Museum of Man)* until 1974. The story of Sara Baartman resurfaced in 1981 when Stephen Jay Gould, a palaeontologist wrote about her story in his book *The Mismeasure of Man* where he criticised racial science.

Following the African National Congress (ANC)'s victory in the South African elections, President Nelson Mandela requested that the French government return the remains of Sara Baartman so that she could be laid to rest. The process took eight years, as the French had to draft a carefully worded bill that would not allow other countries to claim treasures taken by the French. Finally on the sixth of March

2002, Sara Baartman was brought back home to South Africa where she was buried. On 9 August 2002, Women's Day, a public holiday in South Africa, Sara was buried at Hankey in the Eastern Cape Province

Krotoa (Eva)

Krotoa (known as Eva to the Dutch and English settlers) was the niece of Autshumao, a Khoi leader and interpreter to the Dutch (he was known as Harry/Herry first by the English and then by the Dutch).

A young Krotoa, of about 10 or 11 years old, was taken in by Jan van Riebeeck during the first few days of Dutch settlement in the Cape. She worked as a servant to the Commander's wife, Maria van Riebeek (nee de la Quellerie), and is first mentioned in van Riebeeck's diary in January 1654 as 'a girl who had lived with us'. She mastered Dutch and Portuguese and responded eagerly to Christian instruction given her by Maria.

As her command of the Dutch language and her familiarity with Dutch ways grew, so did her usefulness as an interpreter. Krotoa established herself as a staunch friend of the Dutch, negotiating a co-operative relationship between the fort and the followers of her rich relative Oedasoa. She was later instrumental in working out terms for ending the First Dutch-Khoi-khoi War.

In the 1650s Eva was the only figure possessing an intimate knowledge of both Khoikhoi and Dutch culture; as she passed back and forth between one society and the other, she exchanged her Dutch clothing for Khoikhoi skins, and vice versa. However, her work as an interpreter was not easy at this time, as she was torn between her loyalty to the Dutch (who had taken her in and given her new clothes) and her own people (whose land was being taken over by the Dutch in the late 1650s). Due to this dilemma, Krotoa often struggled to maintain trust on both sides.

This struggle is evident in a report by van Riebeeck's diarist, who recorded the words of the Khoi chief and interpreter, Doman: 'I am a Hottentot and not a Dutchman, but you, Eva, try to curry favour with the Commander [van Riebeeck].' Doman therefore saw her as a traitor.

Yet van Riebeeck, who understood that Krotoa was the niece of the Goringhaicona Chief Autshumao (Harry), felt she was overly devoted to her uncle. Ironically it was according to Krotoa's advice (supported by Doman) that van Riebeeck once had Autshumato captured and sent to Robben Island.

In 1662 Krotoa became the first indigenous Southern African to be baptised a Christian, and the Dutch settlers named her Eva. But in the same year, the van Riebeeck's departured the Cape leaving Krotoa feeling vulnerable. She was recommended to van Riebeeck's successor, Wagenaer, but the new Governor was suspicious of her. This was partly because of the fact that she left to visit her people from time to time. Life was also extremely hard for Krotoa after the deaths of both Autshumato and Doman, as she remained the only experienced go-between at the Cape.

On 26 April 1664, Eva's engagement to Danish soldier and explorer Pieter van Meerhof was announced. The announcement came three months after van Meerhof's sixth expedition into the interior. The couple were married on 2 June 1664, at the house of Commander Zacharias Wagenaer. The Company (VOC), which favoured total cultural assimilation for Khoikhoi, gave her a generous dowry. The keeper of Wagenaer's diary noted that this union was "The first marriage contracted here according to Christian usage with a native." As it was only 12 years after van Riebeeck's landing at the Cape, marriages between Whites and Natives were not prohibited at this time.

One year later, Eva, van Meerhof and their 2 children went to live on Robben Island, where van Meerhof was appointed superintendent. His job was to get rid of snakes, spiders and similar creatures. When Krotoa, who gave birth to her third child in 1666 - the family briefly returned to the mainland to baptize the baby. Later, on an expedition to Madagascar, Van Meerhoff was killed in a skirmish.

Krotoa and her children returned to the mainland in September 1668. For a while Eva remained a respectable member of European society, but soon started to drink heavily and turned to prostitution. In February 1669, her drunken behaviour at the dinner table of Commander Wagenaer, and her increasing bitterness against the settlers, prompted a warning from the Dutch that if she did not correct her ways, she would be banished. Krotoa decided to abandon her children and run away, but she was soon taken back to the fort as a prisoner. In March 1669 she was banished to Robben Island for immoral behaviour. She died on the Island 5 years later on 29 July 1674, and was buried the next day in the church of the new Castle.

At her death the Dutch saw her tragic life as proof that Khoikhoi were unable to absorb the best of European culture; *'With the dogs she returned to her own vomit,'* the official diarist recorded, *'a clear illustration that nature, no matter how tightly muzzled by imprinted moral principles ... reverts to its inborn qualities'*

Eva's youngest children, Pieternella and Salamon, who were from her marriage to von Meerhof, were taken to Mauritius in 1677 by a man named Bartholomeus Born. Pieternella later married free burgher

Daniel Saayman and had four sons and four daughters- the second daughter named Eva after her grandmother. Pieternella and her family returned to the Cape in 1709.

Little is known about the lives of Pieternella's brothers and of the children that Krotoa bore out of wedlock.

Joshua Berry

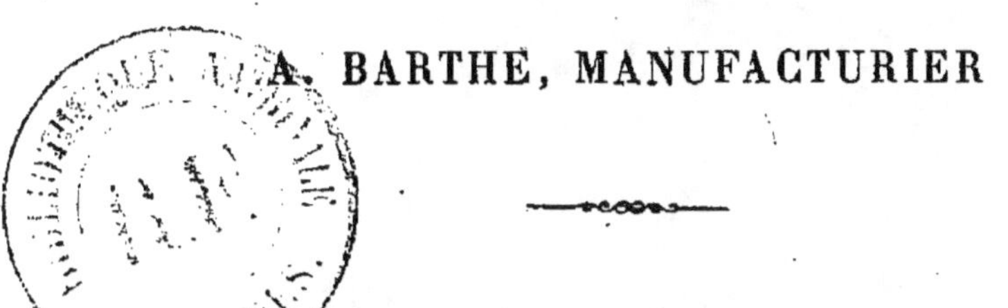

A. BARTHE, MANUFACTURIER

PROGRAMME D'UN PATRIOTE

LE GOUVERNEMENT

DE LA RAISON

BOURGES

IMPRIMERIE ET LITHOGRAPHIE DE A. JOLLET

2, RUE DES ARMURIERS, 2

MARS 1871

L'antipathie, peut-être même la répulsion, qu'é-
prouvent en France beaucoup d'honnêtes gens, et
notamment les populations rurales, pour le gouvernement de la République, m'ont inspiré la pensée
de chercher à éclairer la généralité des masses sur
le véritable sens du mot République, ou plutôt sur
l'interprétation à donner aux principes qui forment
la base de ce gouvernement, trop injustement atta-
qué. Seul, plus que tout autre, il aurait le droit de
se dire d'origine divine, s'il était permis à un gouvernement de revendiquer ce titre. Le fondateur
même du christianisme n'a-t-il pas, en effet, en-
seigné les principes sur lesquels la République base
son édifice.

Le Christ, dans tout ce qu'il a appris aux hommes,
a mis en lumière avec une clarté rare tout ce qu'il
y a de beau et de majestueux dans les principes de
cette institution, et on pourrait dire de lui, s'il était
permis de le faire descendre de son rôle divin aux
choses de ce monde, qu'il s'est montré le plus fer-
vent et fidèle propagateur des idées sur lesquelles
est basée la République.

Hors des libertés que je viens de définir, nulle autre ne peut s'exercer honnêtement qu'à la condition de se conformer rigoureusement aux lois du pays et de respecter les droits d'autrui ; la véritable liberté, a dit Dacier, consistant à n'obéir à aucune passion.

Un peuple n'est digne de jouir de grandes libertés que s'il possède lui-même de grandes vertus, et la première de toutes c'est le respect de la loi, autrement dit, le respect de l'autorité ; l'autorité et la liberté étant deux forces qui doivent toujours s'unir et jamais ne se combattre, l'une étant conservatrice, et l'autre étant conquérante, comme l'a dit avec beaucoup de raison et une grande élévation d'âme, une de nos grandes illustrations, dont le patriotisme vient d'avoir un immense retentissement (1).

Pour ce qui est de respecter les droits d'autrui dans l'exercice de sa propre liberté, la chose découle d'elle-même, il n'y aurait plus de liberté en ne respectant pas celle de son prochain, ce serait vouloir créer l'arbitraire à son profit, tomber dans la licence et, par cela même, fausser le principe sur lequel on voudrait s'appuyer soi-même.

ÉGALITÉ

Ce mot est inexorable ; il porte en lui-même l'abolition de tous les priviléges de la naissance sans

(1) Monseigneur Dupanloup d'Orléans.

exception, et c'est ce que tout esprit juste doit désirer.

On peut descendre d'une noble race, mais être indigne de ses aïeux, et la société ne vous doit rien de ce que vous ne méritez pas.

Travaillez, illustrez-vous comme l'ont fait vos ancêtres et on s'inclinera devant vos vertus, devant votre mérite; mais n'essayez pas de couronner votre front d'un blason que vous n'avez pas gagné, la République le déclarerait sans valeur.

Sous le régime de l'égalité les honneurs et les fonctions deviennent accessibles à tous les citoyens sans distinction de rang : à chacun selon sa capacité, à chaque capacité selon ses œuvres. Montrez-vous digne et capable et la société, sans considérer votre point de départ, vous décernera les récompenses que vous saurez mériter.

Devant la loi aussi nous sommes tous égaux. N'arguez donc pas de votre naissance, de vos titres, de l'inviolabilité de vos fonctions; le principe de l'égalité, qui est inflexible, n'admet que le droit et la cause du juste.

En résumé, l'égalité est la négation de tous les priviléges, autres que ceux que donne le mérite personnel sous toutes les formes. Voilà ma définition.

Mais l'égalité n'entend pas dire que tous les hommes doivent posséder au même degré les biens et les honneurs. La société, s'il en était ainsi, serait troublée dans son harmonie, et, en outre, il faudrait admettre, pour que les choses conservassent leur

entier équilibre, le même esprit d'économie et de conduite chez tous, l'égalité d'aptitude au travail, l'égalité d'intelligence et de mérite, chose entièrement inadmissible.

L'égalité métaphysique n'est donc pas, comme on le voit, celle que nous rêvons. Nous la croirions plutôt nuisible qu'utile à la société ; aussi ne demandons-nous que cette égalité pratique que chacun comprendra d'après nos définitions, et que nous basons sur les droits que donnent les vertus et le mérite de chaque citoyen.

L'intelligence, le travail, la probité, la bonne conduite, qui conduisent aux honneurs et à la fortune, aussi bien le pauvre que le riche, seront et doivent toujours être remarqués et honorés ; les lois de la justice, qui sont immuables, n'admettraient pas qu'il en fût autrement.

FRATERNITÉ

La fraternité est le sentiment qui doit porter l'homme à vivre toujours en bon accord, en bonne amitié, autrement dit à vivre en frère avec son prochain, et à l'encourager à mettre en pratique cette maxime si simple et si juste qui dit de « ne pas faire à autrui ce qu'on ne voudrait pas qu'il vous fît. »

La fraternité a pour sœur aînée la charité, et celle-ci doit être la vertu dominante du vrai républicain, et être toujours son signe distinctif.

La fraternité doit puiser sa véritable force dans l'observance scrupuleuse des principes de l'égalité; car lorsque l'homme se sera pénétré de cette vérité, que nous sommes égaux par la naissance, tout sentiment de sot orgueil qui pourrait le porter à se croire le droit d'exprimer du dédain à autrui, s'éloignera de son esprit, par cela même que ce sentiment sera flétri et condamné par la société.

L'honnêteté donne des droits incontestables à l'estime générale, et je vais plus loin, en disant que tous les mérites, quels qu'ils soient, doivent donner les mêmes droits au respect.

L'homme qui, par son travail et son intelligence, acquiert de la notoriété a droit au respect.

L'homme qui se distingue dans l'agriculture, dans les arts, dans les sciences, dans l'industrie, dans le commerce, dans le métier des armes, dans le clergé, dans la magistrature, a droit au respect.

Et l'homme qui, né pauvre, se voue à un état manuel et l'exerce avec courage et probité, a aussi des droits incontestables au respect de tous, et par cela même qu'il se trouve placé plus bas dans l'échelle sociale, il est plus digne peut-être de l'estime générale, ou tout au moins il mérite plus d'égards de la part de ceux que l'intelligence ou la fortune favorise, sa susceptibilité étant généralement plus grande et ayant habituellement pour mesure le degré de son ignorance ou de son infortune.

J'oserais, en outre, affirmer que le jour où l'homme haut placé, soit par son mérite, soit par le hasard de la naissance, professera avec persévé-

rance de bons sentiments pour la classe laborieuse, plutôt que de lui faire sentir sans cesse sa supériorité, il l'améliorera et obtiendra d'elle le véritable dévouement, qui doit devenir la base du sentiment de la fraternité et lui servir de point d'appui.

Je sais qu'on va me dire : Mais croyez-vous que les hommes sont assez bons pour pratiquer les principes de la République tels que vous venez de les définir ?

Pensez-vous que la société, si souvent ébranlée depuis quatre-vingts ans par les révolutions, aura la vertu et le calme nécessaires pour se renfermer dans le cadre, pourtant déjà bien libéral, que vous venez de lui tracer ?

Pensez-vous que certains hommes, les démagogues, les anarchistes, aspirant au bien-être sans le travail, à l'égalité sans le mérite, reconnaîtront avec vous que la liberté doit avoir un frein, que l'égalité et la fraternité doivent s'arrêter aux abus ?

Cette question peut avoir quelque chose de fondé ; mais je répondrais à ceux qui me l'adresseraient : Défiez-vous d'abord de vous-mêmes plutôt que de ceux que vous craignez. Ne vous laissez pas égarer par votre imagination, qui vous présente trop souvent comme un fantôme redoutable ce qui n'est en réalité qu'un spectre sans consistance. Secouez votre torpeur, armez-vous et résistez, et lorsque vous aurez pris cette fière attitude, et que dans les deux camps on se sera compté, vous aurez obtenu la victoire sans combat.

Les agitateurs sont en petit nombre. Regardons-les en face, mais ne renonçons pas à notre œuvre

de régénération politique, dans la crainte d'une lutte où la force et le bon droit sont de notre côté.

Pour soutenir notre courage, songeons à nos enfants, et disons-nous avec résolution que pour les mettre à l'abri des révolutions périodiques, auxquelles nous les condamnerions fatalement par un retour à la monarchie, nous voulons fonder cette fois la République libérale, pure et honnête, et qu'au besoin, plutôt que de la laisser souiller par un parti que nous répudions, nous scellerons de notre sang les bases sur lesquelles nous voulons l'établir. C'est là, incontestablement, le plus précieux héritage que nous puissions transmettre à nos fils, et il serait bon que tout homme de cœur en fût bien pénétré.

Ayons donc le courage de supporter la liberté, et si dans ses débuts elle a quelques égarements, elle fait de faux pas, redressons-la, mais ne l'abandonnons pas pour cela. Prouvons-lui notre amour par la fidélité, et ne montrons ni découragement ni faiblesse, si un jour elle réclame notre dévouement et notre appui pour l'arracher des mains de quelques énergumènes qui, sous prétexte de l'aimer et de l'adorer, l'étoufferaient dans leurs étreintes.

Non ! ne la laissons pas en leur pouvoir, si nous reconnaissons qu'ils sont indignes de la pratiquer noblement ; mais ne la répudions pas sous ce prétexte, beaucoup trop frivole, que tout le monde ne saura pas l'exercer comme nous la comprenons nous-mêmes, et qu'elle deviendra une arme dangereuse entre leurs mains. Souvenons-nous que nous

représentons la force, parce que nous avons pour nous le nombre, et que rien ne doit nous détourner du noble but que nous poursuivons.

L'homme n'a rien sans la persévérance !... Les sociétés n'obtiennent rien sans la lutte, et vouloir l'éviter, quand il s'agit de défendre des principes salutaires, qui seuls peuvent assurer à la nation, dans un avenir prochain, le repos et la sécurité, serait une défaillance criminelle, une lâcheté coupable.

On doit reconnaître, en jetant ses regards sur le passé, que la monarchie a fait moralement son temps, et que l'empire en a été le dernier mot.

Vouloir restaurer une dynastie serait une faute impardonnable. La France ne se lavera jamais de celle qu'elle a commise en faisant revivre le parti des Bonaparte, et elle en commettrait une tout aussi cruelle en faisant renaître aujourd'hui un autre prétendant.

Quelles que soient les sympathies très naturelles et très avouables, d'ailleurs, que puisse éveiller dans les cœurs une famille qui, en quittant le trône de France, a laissé de bons souvenirs dans le pays, je n'hésite pas à me prononcer contre elle, parce que en elle je ne vois pas les hommes, je ne vois que le principe.

Si le parti monarchique, en France, ne comptait pas de si nombreux prétendants, je ne verrais pas le même écueil pour le pays à revenir à une monarchie constitutionnelle ; mais, avec la mobilité de l'esprit français, il faut de suite se reporter à la fin

d'un règne, quel qu'honorable qu'il puisse être, et voir ce qui lui succédera.

Sans être bien clairvoyant, la réponse est facile à faire. C'est la révolution d'abord, la République le lendemain.

La conservera-t-on cette fois ?

Oui... Non...

Nul ne peut le prédire.

Nous éprouvons des défaillances ; comme nous, nos fils en éprouveront peut-être aussi. Ils se ressentiront, c'est à craindre, de l'éducation qu'ils reçoivent, de notre manque d'énergie, de ce défaut de virilité politique qui paralyse tous nos bons sentiments, et rien ne peut nous faire pressentir quelle sera leur conduite.

S'ils restaurent à leur tour une monarchie, on peut cependant préjuger que, Français comme nous, ce ne sera plus avec la famille qui viendra de s'éteindre, mais avec un prince que le peuple rappellera encore de l'exil. Et alors, de révolution en révolution, de catastrophe en catastrophe, la France en pleine décadence tombera dans l'abîme, et elle n'en sortira, s'il lui reste encore assez de vie, que par un bond sublime de la liberté.

Devant une telle perspective, notre devoir est tout tracé. Nous devons éviter à notre pays toutes ces calamités, et nous le pouvons en adoptant aujourd'hui franchement le gouvernement de la République libérale : honnête, laborieuse et tolérante, pour se concilier tous les partis : forte, énergique et puissante, pour pouvoir réprimer sévèrement

toutes les tentatives de désordre et arrêter dans leurs élans irréfléchis certains hommes qui, pleins de bonne foi peut-être, s'imaginent sauver le pays par un culte exalté des institutions démocratiques, et le conduisent, sans s'en douter, tout droit à sa ruine.

Trancher la question dans ce sens, c'est résoudre d'un seul coup le grand problème social qui nous agite, et j'ai la ferme confiance que les hommes qui tiennent dans leurs mains les destinées de la France trouveront dans la solution que j'indique le moyen de donner le calme et la sécurité à tous les esprits, et celui de satisfaire tous les graves intérêts qui viennent de leur être confiés.

Douter de la réalisation de ce programme, qui porte en lui-même l'avenir de la nation, c'est douter de la vérité; et les douteurs sont ceux qui de tout temps ont causé le plus grand mal aux sociétés, en empêchant les institutions les plus belles et les plus sages de s'acclimater et de prendre racine, souvent même dans le sol le meilleur. Et pensez-vous que les vérités se défendent toutes seules? Hélas! il n'en est pas ainsi avec notre pauvre humanité, et la République, qui jusqu'ici n'a pu se faire jour, en est une preuve éclatante.

Aidez donc et fortifiez par votre foi ceux que l'ignorance ou la faiblesse pousse à la défaillance; mais ne doutez jamais vous-même du triomphe des idées justes.

Manquer de conviction, dans la situation doulou-reuse où le pays se trouve, c'est manquer de cœur

et de patriotisme ; mais oser dire qu'un peuple doit gémir sous les fers du despotisme, sous le prétexte qu'une infime minorité est indigne de jouir avec calme de la liberté, c'est fouler aux pieds les droits les plus sacrés de la nation, manquer à ses devoirs et tromper sa conscience.

Comment ! vous reconnaîtriez avec nous que la République est de tous les gouvernements le meilleur, le seul qui puisse nous procurer de grandes économies, et nous permettre de nous relever de nos malheurs, et aussitôt vous ajouteriez à ces paroles pleines d'espérance ce correctif perfide que « c'est un gouvernement trop théorique, d'un fonctionnement presque impossible, somme toute, un rêve irréalisable. »

Mais songez donc que ce langage serait plein de danger. Refuser à un peuple tombé dans l'adversité les moyens de s'en relever, ce serait décréter sciemment sa mort. Ah ! quelle responsabilité, grand Dieu, porteraient devant la postérité ceux qui auraient agi de la sorte.

Vous n'ignorez pas plus que nous, messieurs nos contradicteurs, que sous l'antiquité et le moyen-âge, des peuples qui étaient loin d'avoir notre génie vivaient en République, et s'en trouvaient heureux ; que, de nos jours, le peuple américain, qui souvent a été l'objet de notre admiration, vit aussi en République, et que tout près de nous la Suisse, ce pays florissant et hospitalier, est un pays républicain. Et d'où vient que la France ne pourrait pas vivre, elle aussi, sous cette grande forme de gou-

vernement, lorsque ses aspirations, ses plus chers intérêts, son avenir, tout en un mot l'y convie?

Voulez-vous nous le dire?

Et voulez-vous nous dire aussi pourquoi au lieu de rester sur la brèche pour rassurer les bons et combattre les agitateurs, vous fuyez d'épouvante au premier souffle des révolutions, lorsque le peuple frémissant d'impatience, vous réclame les libertés qu'il serait si sage et si simple de lui accorder?

Et pourquoi, dans ces moments d'effervescence, allez-vous demander asile à un pays voisin qui vit en République, lorsque vous attaquez si sévèrement cette institution dans votre propre pays?

La Suisse, direz-vous, est un pays sage, et chez elle nous trouvons la sécurité et la protection d'un gouvernement honnête.

Voyez jusque où va votre inconséquence. Vous glorifiez ailleurs ce que vous condamnez chez vous, et tout cela pourquoi?

Parce que vous aimez la liberté, mais que vous voudriez l'obtenir sans le plus léger sacrifice fait à votre repos. Vous l'aimez, c'est vrai, mais vous voudriez laisser à vos enfants, sous le prétexte que les événements auraient le temps de les mûrir davantage et de les former progressivement aux idées libérales, les dangers que vous craignez qu'il y ait à courir pour vous-mêmes dans l'usage immédiat d'un tel régime; en un mot, au lieu d'agir en pères de famille, vous obéissez à l'égoïsme le plus coupable, voilà la vérité.

La peur a toujours poussé l'homme aux plus

2

grandes aberrations d'esprit, et vous subissez sa domination. Mais, de grâce, repoussez loin de vous ces craintes chimériques ; il n'existe nulle part de dangers sérieux si ce n'est ceux qui résultent de votre inertie.

Vous redoutez donc que la République nous ramène aux excès de 1793, et ne fasse couler un sang innocent : mais réfléchissez que les temps ne sont plus les mêmes. Lorsque le 4 août 1789 une Assemblée nationale abolissait le régime féodal, et donnait à un peuple, jusque là opprimé sous le plus cruel despotisme, le premier signal de son émancipation politique, il était inévitable que ce nouveau régime amènerait ses excès ; mais croyez-vous donc que les révolutions qui se sont succédé depuis n'aient rien appris à la nation ? Pensez-vous que l'immense majorité de ce peuple, qui est honnête et laborieuse, et ne demande que l'ordre, ne comprend pas elle-même que la liberté ne peut régner qu'à l'ombre d'un pouvoir fort et respecté ? Et croyez-vous enfin que les jours néfastes que nous venons de traverser n'amèneront pas la nation au recueillement, lorsque ses premières émotions se seront calmées ?

Je sais que notre nature ardente, qui nous porte à la légèreté, peut nous faire commettre bien des fautes, mais la leçon que la France vient de recevoir est cependant trop cruelle pour ne pas en attendre une amélioration dans ses mœurs politiques ; entrons donc courageusement dans les réformes de toute nature ; à ce prix seulement le pays peut être sauvé.

Le peuple a appris aujourd'hui à ses cruels dépens que toutes les monarchies nous conduisent infailliblement au même résultat : c'est toujours dans l'abîme des révolutions qu'elle nous plongent, ou la guerre avec l'invasion du territoire qu'elles nous ramènent.

Un pays finit par s'épuiser dans la lutte, et le nôtre ne subirait pas impunément une fois encore l'épreuve douloureuse qu'il vient de traverser ; les plaies de la France sont béantes, il faut les refermer promptement. Que le peuple apprenne donc aujourd'hui, par une voix amie, que le moment est venu de se prononcer résolument contre toute restauration monarchique. La République seule peut relever le pays de sa chute, elle seule peut rallier tous les partis, maintenir l'ordre, et nous préserver de tout retour aux révolutions.

Que les hommes d'ordre et de bons sens de tous les partis renoncent donc à faire revivre leurs prétendants déchus, il le faut pour sauver le pays, et en s'obstinant davantage à vouloir faire triompher une politique égoïste et surannée, ce serait vouer la France aux plus effroyables malheurs.

Que tous les esprits, du reste, se rassurent, et que ceux qui, dans la crainte du désordre, ont systématiquement combattu jusqu'ici la République, que nous réclamons pour notre pays, sachent bien que, comme eux, nous voulons la tranquillité pour ramener partout la confiance et le travail, convaincu que la prospérité et la gloire ne reviendront à nous qu'à ce prix.

Prêtons-nous donc un mutuel appui, au lieu de nous combattre, et suivons en cela le noble exemple qui nous est donné par les hommes qui nous gouvernent ; ils ont compris que rien n'était possible sans la conciliation, et la conciliation est devenue aussitôt leur drapeau, leur mot d'ordre.

En nous unissant, nous aussi, nous donnerons au Gouvernement la force morale qui lui est nécessaire, et nous le placerons au-dessus de tous les dangers.

En nous unissant, nous lui permettrons de réaliser promptement des économies considérables sur toutes nos administrations, et d'arriver graduellement à la diminution de l'impôt, ce qui est le vœu le plus ardent de la nation. Et ce résultat, qui dépend tout de notre bon accord, de notre entente, peut être obtenu si rapidement que nous nous libèrerons, à n'en pas douter, du terrible impôt de guerre que nous venons de subir, sans que le pays en ressente aucune cruelle privation.

Pénétrons-nous donc bien de cette vérité, que le gouvernement de la République est, de tous, celui qui nous coûtera le meilleur marché. C'est lui qui supprime tous les gros traitements, tous les fonctionnaires inutiles, qui réduit les gros bataillons, qui fait cesser, en un mot, tous les abus qui ont pour conséquence d'écraser le peuple d'impôts au profit de quelques-uns seulement qui élèvent à côté de lui des fortunes scandaleuses.

En nous unissant, enfin, la République, qui deviendra notre drapeau commun, nous ramènera la

force et avec elle notre ancien prestige et toute notre gloire. La France reprendra alors sa juste prépondérance, nécessaire au repos du monde; elle sera devenue désormais un peuple invincible.

Après avoir fait appel à la conciliation de tous les partis indistinctement, pour fonder une sage République, on est en droit de me demander de formuler mes idées sur la meilleure organisation à donner à ce gouvernement.

Cette demande me paraît juste, et je vais y satisfaire d'une manière brève et rapide tout en m'efforçant d'apporter dans le développement de mes idées le plus de clarté possible.

La première question qui se présente à l'examen, et qui aussi offre le plus d'importance, est le *suffrage universel*. Je n'y toucherai qu'avec une excessive réserve, sachant combien ce sujet est délicat à traiter.

Néanmoins, j'examinerai, après l'avoir définie, si cette institution a toujours été pratiquée avec loyauté, et je signalerai les abus qu'on en a pu faire.

Qui dit suffrage universel, dit : libre émanation de la volonté de l'homme dans l'ordre politique.

Toute atteinte portée à la liberté de l'électeur, dans l'exercice de son droit, fausse donc le principe, et doit être considérée comme une offense faite aux lois de la morale.

Le suffrage universel doit être la base fondamentale de la République; je dirai même mieux : il doit en être le principe vital.

Il est sacré, comme étant la seule arme puissante

et pacifique des peuples, et nul ne devrait s'en servir que pour en faire un noble et loyal usage.

Est-ce ainsi qu'agissaient les monarques et ceux qui ont eu la secrète ambition de le devenir?

Sans hésitation, on peut répondre non.

Disposant du pouvoir et de l'argent, et ajoutant à cette double force le prestige que le nom exerce sur les masses, ils se servent de cette institution populaire pour la faire tourner à leur profit, étant toujours beaucoup plus préoccupés de leurs intérêts personnels ou dynastiques que de ceux de la nation.

Je conclus de là, que le suffrage universel, tel qu'il se pratique aujourd'hui, sera toujours une arme formidable dans les mains des adversaires de la République, mais qu'il ne donnera jamais à celle-ci un appui sérieux et efficace. La puissance et les ressorts nombreux que donne l'ambition individuelle lui manquent, et cela suffit pour la placer toujours dans une situation d'infériorité notable.

Quel contre-poids opposera-t-on à cette force pour rétablir un juste équilibre?

Que fera-t-on pour déjouer les manœuvres coupables et dérouter l'intrigue?

En un mot, que faut-il faire pour que le suffrage universel devienne l'expression réelle ou voisine de la vérité, et pour qu'il conserve toute la majesté de l'indépendance?

Le remède est unique... Il faut apporter une modification dans l'expression du suffrage, en se gardant avec soin d'en altérer le principe.

On a parlé beaucoup du système qui consisterait à exiger de tout électeur une instruction élémentaire qui le rendît apte à comprendre l'acte important que la société lui demande d'accomplir. Sans contredit, c'est la solution qui serait la plus désirable ; mais en tenant compte de la quantité énorme de gens illettrés qui existe aujourd'hui en France, on doit sagement renoncer à cette combinaison, en laissant à nos enfants le soin de décider ce qu'il y aura à faire lorsque l'instruction gratuite et obligatoire, qui va être indubitablement décrétée par le gouvernement de la République, aura pu répandre ses bienfaits sur les masses.

Vouloir mettre ce système en pratique dans les circonstances actuelles, ce serait vouloir la suppression du suffrage universel, pour faire revivre le cens électoral au profit des hommes instruits ; et comme je connais tous les dangers qu'il y aurait à toucher à cette institution, qui est passée dans les mœurs du pays, j'écarte vite cette idée, bien qu'elle puisse paraître fort raisonnable à certains esprits, pour donner mon exclusive préférence à un autre système, qui consisterait à restreindre le suffrage universel à la commune, ce qui donnerait lieu autrement dit au *suffrage à deux degrés.* Celui-ci est le seul qui soit réellement pratique dans les temps où nous vivons. Il laisse intact le principe du suffrage universel, le met à l'abri des plus gros dangers et lui donne l'esprit de discernement qui lui manque totalement aujourd'hui.

Je vais de suite en expliquer le mécanisme. Mais,

avant toute chose, je demande qu'on admette avec moi un point essentiel qui fait la force de ce système: c'est que dans une commune tout homme qui a un mérite quelconque y est vite connu et apprécié de tout le monde, aussi bien par le paysan illettré que par les plus érudits.

Partant de ce point, que je considère désormais comme un axiôme, je demande l'élection à deux degrés pour les conseillers d'arrondissement, les conseillers généraux et les députés.

Quant aux conseillers municipaux, ils seront élus de la même manière qu'aujourd'hui. Il ressort de mon système que rien n'est changé à leur élection.

Chaque fois qu'une élection aurait lieu, le peuple tout entier, sans autre exclusion que celle que porte la loi, serait appelé à y prendre part pour élire ses électeurs, et ceux-ci à leur tour auraient à nommer, huit jours après, nos représentants, nos conseillers généraux, nos conseillers d'arrondissement.

Quel nombre d'électeurs faudrait-il adopter? Je laisse à d'autres plus expérimentés que moi le soin de résoudre cette question; mais, à titre d'avis, je crois qu'on ne devrait pas dépasser le chiffre de 2 à 3 p. 100 des votants inscrits, et cela afin de donner aux électeurs toutes les facilités voulues pour se réunir au chef-lieu de canton, où le vote aurait lieu, pour y étudier et discuter sérieusement le mérite de chaque candidat.

L'élection ainsi pratiquée aurait divers avantages. Le premier de tous serait de conserver au peuple

la jouissance du suffrage universel, toutes les fois qu'il y aurait à en faire usage.

Le second, celui de remettre en des mains éclairées et généralement impartiales, le choix d'élire les représentants auxquels la nation confie ses destinées.

Et le troisième, le plus précieux de tous peut-être, serait celui d'éloigner du scrutin, dans une bonne mesure au moins, si ce n'est radicalement, toutes les influences nuisibles, toutes les intrigues dangereuses.

Certains partisans de l'élection à deux degrés proposent de remettre dans les mains de nos conseillers municipaux le droit de faire toutes nos élections.

Je ne suis pas de cet avis, et pour divers motifs :

Le premier, parce que dans un conseil municipal les hommes qui le composent ont de trop fréquentes occasions de se réunir, et que de ce contact réitéré il pourrait naître des coteries dangereuses pour l'indépendance des élections.

Le second, parce que ce serait donner un caractère politique à des hommes dont le rôle doit se limiter exclusivement aux affaires de la commune, ce qui pourrait les entraîner à négliger et compromettre des intérêts respectables sans aucune compensation pour le pays.

Et le troisième, parce que ce serait tenir éloigné du scrutin, pendant un temps trop long, le peuple dont l'intervention est indispensable, à tous les titres, chaque fois qu'il y a élire les représentants de nos diverses assemblées.

Cette question importante du suffrage universel
étant résolue, je vais sur cette base, et d'une manière rapide, développer mon programme.

Et, tout d'abord, je commence par donner au
pays une assemblée nationale à laquelle le peuple
remet ses pouvoirs soŭverains.

Au lieu de 750 députés, je n'en nomme que 600
au maximum. Je trouve ce nombre amplement suf-
fisant.

L'assemblée élue se constitue, nomme son président, ses secrétaires, ses bureaux, et nomme enfin,
en le prenant dans l'assemblée même, comme pour
rendre hommage à la souveraineté du suffrage universel, le président de la République, que j'appel-
lerai, pour me conformer au sentiment de notre
chambre actuelle, le « président du conseil des ministres, chef dŭ pouvoir exécutif. »

Ce chef du pouvoir exécutif est élu pour un temps
illimité ; mais il est toujours révocable par un vote
de l'assemblée.

Ce système, que l'éminent M. Grévy, président
de notre assemblée actuelle, a préconisé en 1848,
dans un amendement resté célèbre, est également
le mien, et je lui cède respectueusement la défense
de son idée, en reproduisant les paroles textuelles
qu'il prononça, il y a vingt-trois ans, à l'assemblée
constituante : « Le seul fait de l'élection populaire

donnera au président de la République une force excessive. Oubliez-vous que ce sont les électeurs de l'an X qui ont donné à Bonaparte la force de relever le trône, et de s'y asseoir ! Voilà le pouvoir que vous élevez, et vous dites que vous voulez fonder une République monarchique ! Que feriez-vous de plus, si vous vouliez, sous un nom différent, restaurer la monarchie ? » L'honorable M. Grévy voyait les choses d'un œil juste. On sait que les événements ont justifié ses prévisions.

Il est difficile d'admettre, en effet, que deux pouvoirs issus de l'élection populaire, dont l'un a pour mission de contrôler l'autre, aient assez de vertu pour vivre toujours dans la plus parfaite harmonie, alors qu'ils se sentent une égale puissance, et que l'un d'eux se trouve personnifié dans un seul homme. Des conflits incessants doivent naître du frottement de ces deux forces, par la tendance naturelle que doit avoir l'une d'elles à dominer l'autre. Et le pays, qui veut le calme pour rétablir le crédit et la fortune, peut se voir ainsi plongé de nouveau dans les agitations.

Il y a donc un intérêt de première nécessité à écarter avec soin toutes les causes qui pourraient amener de nouvelles discordes, et nous pensons que par l'adoption du système Grévy, le but peut être facilement atteint. La France se prononcera, et si l'esprit public est avec nous, elle n'aura qu'à déclarer que ce qui a été fait par l'assemblée actuelle a été bien fait, et doit être maintenu par la future assemblée constituante. Ce sera alors un grand pas de

fait dans la voie du suffrage à deux degrés, et peut-
être cela suffira-t-il pour en assurer le triomphe?

Le chef du pouvoir exécutif, qui sera une des
premières et des plus populaires illustrations de la
France, aura pour obligation impérieuse, il est vrai,
de marcher d'accord avec l'esprit de la nation ; mais
c'est là justement ce qui fera sa force, et c'est à cela
que nous devons le plus applaudir. C'est résoudre,
en effet, de la manière la plus heureuse, le plus
grand problème qui puisse s'offrir à un peuple, que
de lui donner un chef qui soit obligé de tenir
compte de ses besoins et de ses aspirations. C'est
le moyen le plus sûr de resserrer entre eux les liens
qui doivent toujours les unir ; et de cette entente
cordiale il ne peut résulter que deux grands bienfaits : le bonheur pour le peuple, — la confiance,
l'estime et le respect pour le chef.

Nous devons ajouter ici que nous n'entendons
pas mesurer avec parcimonie les pouvoirs qui doivent être donnés au chef de la République. Il faut
qu'il ait l'initiative la plus grande dans toutes les
questions, qu'il soit revêtu de l'autorité la plus
complète ; qu'en un mot, il jouisse du prestige et
de la force que tout chef d'une grande nation doit
avoir dans les mains, pour faire respecter au de-
hors sa parole, au-dedans les lois du pays, et par
cela même que ce chef est toujours révocable, s'il
fait mal, nous ne devons lui refuser aucun des
moyens de faire le bien.

Ce chef du pouvoir exécutif nomme lui-même
ses ministres ; mais il les choisit dans l'assemblée,

pour ne prendre que des hommes déjà désignés par le suffrage universel.

Les ministres sont responsables de leurs actes devant l'Assemblée, et le jour où celle-ci ne leur témoigne plus sa confiance, ils se retirent et le chef du pouvoir exécutif en nomme d'autres en s'inspirant le plus possible des sentiments de la Chambre, de manière à ne pas se séparer d'elle sur ce point délicat, qui pourrait amener, si l'on n'y prenait garde, de part et d'autre, des froissements assez nombreux. La chute du cabinet ministériel n'entraînera pas, il est vrai, celle de son président, pas plus qu'elle n'entraîne celle du monarque sous une monarchie constitutionnelle, mais son influence morale pourrait se voir amoindrie, ce qui déjà serait fort regrettable.

Afin de donner à ce gouvernement, que je viens de décrire, toute la stabilité possible, ce qui ne peut être obtenu que si on écarte avec soin toutes les causes de révolution, je remets à l'Assemblée nationale des pouvoirs souverains et permanents, et pour cela je propose de n'en renouveler les membres que tous les trois ans et par tiers. Les renouvellements se feraient d'après une division territoriale, et les deux premiers auraient lieu par voie de tirage au sort, à cause de la différence de durée dans le mandat des membres de la première assemblée élue.

Bien que tous ceux qui jusqu'ici ont traité du régime représentatif aient toujours reconnu la nécessité d'une seconde Chambre, je crois qu'il est possible de s'en passer sans préjudice pour la nation.

Nous avons vu, en effet, combien ce Sénat, si coûteux sous l'Empire, a rendu peu de services au pays, et nous nous souvenons tous de l'état de discrédit dans lequel il avait fini par tomber, malgré l'illustration incontestable de beaucoup de ses membres.

Une seconde Chambre destinée à pondérer les pouvoirs de l'Assemblée représentative et à vérifier si dans tous ses actes les conditions de constitutionnalité sont rigoureusement observées, paraît avoir sans doute son caractère d'utilité, mais reconnaissons que si cette utilité paraît réelle ce n'est que parce qu'il est admis que la nation peut commettre des erreurs graves dans le choix de ses représentants. Mais si pour un instant nous supprimons par la pensée le danger, alors cesse aussi la nécessité de cette seconde Chambre ; elle n'est plus qu'une superfétation coûteuse, un rouage inutile.

Examinons donc s'il est raisonnable de croire que le suffrage à deux degrés puisse préserver la nation des graves erreurs prévues.

Pour moi, cela ne fait aucun doute.

Parce que j'admets comme une chose sûre que lorsqu'il s'agira de nommer de simples électeurs, l'opinion publique des communes ne fera jamais fausse route. Ce qui l'égare aujourd'hui, c'est l'ignorance du mérite des candidats à nommer, ce sont les intrigues, ce sont les passions anarchiques ou réactionnaires qui agissent violemment sur elle ; mais lorsqu'il n'y aura plus qu'à choisir dans le sein de la commune des hommes honnêtes et de bon sens, oh ! alors le peuple lui-même fera son

choix, et il le fera, j'en réponds, avec une rectitude
de coup-d'œil qui surprendra bien des personnes,
et ce qui est pour moi une garantie de plus que les
choses se passeront comme je le dis, c'est que ni
les rancunes de clocher, ni les colères ne viendront
nullement se mêler à ces élections, à cause [même
du caractère essentiellement éphémère qu'il s'agira
de décerner aux électeurs. D'un côté, le mobile de
l'ambition sera presque nul ; de l'autre, la crainte
de voir grandir son voisin, en lui créant un privi-
lége durable, n'aura pas sa raison d'être.

Partant maintenant de ce point que les électeurs
qui seraient désignés par le suffrage universel pour
nommer nos représentants, seront tous des hommes
loyaux ayant l'instruction ou à défaut le bon sens,
je ne puis admettre à aucun titre que la nation
puisse se tromper assez gravement pour envoyer
dans une chambre une majorité d'hommes qui
n'aurait pas le degré voulu de sagesse et de raison
pour diriger les intérêts de la nation ; surtout lorsque nous raisonnons avec cette donnée que, dans
un sentiment général de conciliation, et pour donner
à la France le repos et le bonheur, nos adversaires
d'aujourd'hui auront renoncé à leurs sympathies
politiques pour accepter loyalement le gouvernement de la République comme celui que la raison
nous impose.

On doit conclure, au contraire, de ce qui vient
d'être dit, que tous nos représentants seront minu-
tieusement discutés un à un, et qu'il résultera de
la sévérité de ce choix une chambre composée de

tous les hommes d'élite du pays. Aussi oserais-je dire qu'il serait plutôt juste de décerner à une pareille assemblée un brevet d'infaillibilité, que de la croire capable de commettre des erreurs graves, et de jeter le pays dans une fausse voie. Non , ces hommes, j'en réponds, auront la raison de résister à tous les entraînements dangereux, et, s'inspirant de la grandeur et de la responsabilité de leur mandat, tous leurs actes porteront le sceau de la plus profonde sagesse. En un mot, ils seront de véritables conservateurs, et alors, à l'exemple de Rome la républicaine qui n'avait qu'un Sénat, la France elle aussi n'aura qu'une Assemblée, mais elle pourra en être fière.

Et maintenant, que ceux qui m'auront fait l'honneur de lire cet opuscule, me fassent aussi l'honneur de croire que je n'ai pas la naïveté de penser que tout doit fonctionner sans obstacle dans la pratique d'un gouvernement tel que je viens de le définir. J'ai assez l'expérience des hommes, comme ayant toujours vécu à leur contact immédiat, pour ne pas me nourrir de cette illusion, et pour savoir la part qu'on doit faire aux passions et à la faiblesse humaine ; mais je suis de ceux qui veulent qu'on ne s'arrête pas devant toutes les difficultés, sous prétexte qu'elles sont insurmontables. Ce sont ces craintes-là qui étouffent le progrès, qui arrêtent les peuples dans leur marche, et ce serait justice, peut-être, que de vouer au mépris du pays ceux qui, sciemment et dans un sentiment de pur égoïsme, entretiennent des idées de défiance dans le courant populaire.

J'ai accompli ici ma tâche, et je la résume.

J'ai commencé tout d'abord par définir dans un sens libéral et honnête les trois principes : *Liberté, Egalité, Fraternité*, et sur eux j'ai basé une République sage.

Cela fait, j'ai cherché à écarter toutes les craintes des pessimistes, et pour cela j'ai encouragé à une vaillante résistance tous les hommes d'ordre et de travail qui veulent s'opposer, avec raison, au développement des idées anarchiques, que quelques personnes égarées ont le fol espoir de faire triompher.

Ici j'ajouterai, comme simple observation, que .c'est à tort qu'on confond souvent la République avec la révolution. La République n'a aucune alliance avec cette dernière, pas plus que n'en avaient les diverses monarchies qui ont péri sous ses efforts. Mais ne grossissons pas le fantôme, et soyons convaincus, parce que c'est la vérité, qu'un grand nombre de ceux qu'on suppose être des révolutionnaires ne le sont pas en réalité. Ils veulent simplement la République, et ils se rallieront de suite sous son drapeau pour y vivre paisiblement le jour où ils auront la confiance que le pays accepte d'une manière définitive ce mode de gouvernement. S'ils combattent donc aujourd'hui dans les rangs des ennemis de l'ordre, c'est qu'ils y sont poussés par les

violences de certains réactionnaires qui, par respect pour leur propre nom, si ce n'est par amour du pays, devraient dans ces moments de déchirement nous donner l'exemple du calme et de la dignité, et qu'ensuite ils croient voir partout dans leur égarement des ennemis de la République, même où il n'en existe pas.

Devant la patrie en danger faisons cesser vite tout malentendu, et pour cela déclarons que la République est désormais le gouvernement de la nation, et si, après cette déclaration faite solennellement, il existe encore debout et armés des hommes égarés, oh! alors plus d'hésitation, combattons-les à outrance, et montrons-leur une fois pour toutes qu'un citoyen ne fait pas la loi à mille.

Je reprends mon examen rétrospectif pour dire que je me suis appliqué à faire ressortir l'impossibilité de tout retour à la monarchie, en m'appuyant sur ce que l'esprit français, élevé et nourri dans l'étude des idées de 1789, ne consentirait jamais à restaurer *volontairement* le principe d'hérédité au trône, et en m'appuyant aussi sur ce que la monarchie était représentée aujourd'hui par des *prétendants trop nombreux* pour qu'aucun d'eux pût nous donner, même avec la meilleure volonté, un gage sérieux de stabilité et de sécurité pour l'avenir.

J'ai exposé plus loin que la République était le meilleur gouvernement de tous, que lui seul pouvait nous ramener la prospérité et la gloire; et, m'appuyant sur cette conviction, j'ai fait appel à

la conciliation de tous les partis indistinctement, en les suppliant d'accepter au nom de la France en danger, cette seule institution possible que je nomme *le Gouvernement de la raison.*

J'ai enfin terminé ce travail en formulant mes idées sur la meilleure organisation à donner à ce gouvernement, et j'ai insisté particulièrement sur un nouveau système de suffrage universel dit suffrage à deux degrés, dont l'expérience a déjà montré en d'autres temps la supériorité.

Je dois faire remarquer également que pour donner un gage sérieux de stabilité à la République, j'ai proposé de lui donner une Chambre dont les pouvoirs seraient permanents. C'est un moyen de ne jamais laisser le pays sans gouvernement, ne serait-ce même que vingt-quatre heures, et c'est donner satisfaction, dans une large mesure, à ceux qui jusqu'ici n'ont donné la préférence à la monarchie constitutionnelle sur la République qu'à cause du principe d'hérédité que la première possède et que celle-ci n'a pas. Je fais observer seulement que dans le système que je propose c'est une Chambre composée de 600 hommes d'élite que je fais la gardienne vigilante des pouvoirs de la nation, tandis que dans la monarchie c'est à un seul homme qu'on les remet.

BOURGES. — TYPOGRAPHIE DE A. JOLLET.